Susan Isaacs

by the same author

THE EDUCATION OF YOUNG CHILDREN
LONG TERM RESULTS OF INFANT SCHOOL METHODS
EXPERIMENT AND TRADITION IN PRIMARY SCHOOLS

Susan Isaacs

D. E. M. Gardner, M.A.

formerly Reader in Child Development
University of London Institute of Education

Methuen Educational Ltd

LONDON · TORONTO · SYDNEY · WELLINGTON

First published 1969
by Methuen Educational Ltd
11 New Fetter Lane, London EC 4
© *D. E. M. Gardner 1969*

Printed in Great Britain by
Cox & Wyman Ltd.
London, Fakenham and Reading

SBN 423 41980 3

Foreword

When Susan rang me up and told me that she was ill and was going to die I was very angry. She reminded me of my angry reaction a year later when I saw her for the last time.

It seemed such a waste, that this very real and active person should cease to be, simply because of a cancer.

Susan and I got to know each other when we were both students at the Institute of Psycho-Analysis, in the mid-thirties. She had already done her basic work at the Malting House School, and it was about at that time that the Child Development Department of the Institute of Education was created for her. As a psycho-analyst she was having a second training, having become dissatisfied with her first, and this meant a second analysis and a new personal upheaval.

It was of great importance to me that Susan invited me to give a series of lectures each year to her students in the Child Development Course. I was more than surprised. She simply let me loose, in spite of my immaturities, and for some years I lectured to her students out of my paediatric experience. Gradually these lectures developed into a series, ten each year, attempting to cover the subject of the emotional development of the individual. Not only was it kind of Susan to invite me and to leave me to evolve my own method and viewpoint, but also it may have been quite brilliant of her to see that such a use of a colleague could possibly lead to anything at all. But this was typical of her. She was quite outstandingly superior, generous, and at the same time human, vulnerable, modest, and humorously tolerant. When I heard Nathan ruthlessly criticize her ideas and formulations I felt maddened, but I found that she valued exactly this from him and that she made positive use of his ruthlessness, as of his terrific intellect.

It fell to my lot to supply child cases for Susan's child analysis training, and I watched with interest her sensitive management of the total family situation, a difficult thing when one is engaged in learning while carrying out a psycho-analytic treatment involving daily sessions over years. I never had qualms about the course of these treatments, although in those days we worked in a potentially hostile environment.

Of course, if I had known that illness would come and cut short our friendship I would have forged ahead, making much more use than I did of all that she had to offer; but there seemed to be plenty of time; and in any case we all needed to recover from the war.

Then the life of this sturdy soul came to an end, and we who survived were left angry. This memoir compiled by Dorothy Gardner gives me a moment of happiness in that it recaptures some of the reality of a truly great person, one who has had a tremendous influence for good on the attitude of parents and of teachers to the children in their care. This attempt at a reconstruction will serve its purpose if it brings Susan alive to those who never knew her, so that some may feel inclined to read her books by being introduced to her as a struggling, striving, and radiant human being, one who seemed destined to achieve something significant that we cannot now define because her death stopped the process. There is still room for the study of what she actually achieved.

D. W. WINNICOTT, F.R.C.P.

9th September 1968

6

Contents

Preface

In October 1948, Susan's husband, Nathan Isaacs, asked me to write this book as soon as I should retire from my post. I succeeded Susan Isaacs as Head of the Department of Child Development at the University of London Institute of Education in 1943. Professor Jack Tizard, who succeeded me in that position in 1964, has also given me warm encouragement to undertake this task – but I did not actually retire from active work in the department until April 1968, and so this book is appearing more than twenty years after Susan's death.

The loss of Nathan Isaacs has been a tragic handicap, but he gave me much help for many years and collected data for me. I am also greatly indebted to others who are not now living because, knowing I should one day wish to write this book, I have sought contacts with as many people as I could among those who knew Susan Isaacs at different periods of her life and whose names appear in the text. To the many living people who have helped me I wish to offer my warm thanks. They have contributed in many ways: some by reading my manuscript and giving me their advice on it; others by granting interviews or informal meetings to tell me what they knew of Susan Isaacs; and still others who have written to me, given me access to their published articles, or put me in touch with further sources of information. I list their names below, asking indulgence from those who may recognize their contributions to this book but find their names not mentioned. Twenty years is a long time, and even before that many people had talked to me about Susan Isaacs.

My wish to write this book springs from more than a desire

to keep a promise. During many years I have steadily received requests for biographical material about Susan Isaacs from those who, having become very interested in her writings, wished to know about her as a person. Moreover, there has never been a year since Susan's death when my own students have not asked me to give a talk about her and her life. They were experienced teachers and lecturers; but other requests have come also from much younger students in the Colleges of Education. It seemed clear, therefore, that a book would be welcomed by many people who, knowing her work and aware of her tremendous contribution to our understanding of children, feel they want to know more of Susan Isaacs herself, about whom no book has yet been written. For that reason I am glad that Nathan Isaacs wanted me to tell the story of her life and not only of her professional career.

It is possible too that this book may attract some readers who do not know Susan Isaacs' writings, but who are interested in human personality. To these readers the book may be of service if it leads them to her writings where they will find much that will deepen their understanding.

In writing of Susan Isaacs, I have often thought of Florence Nightingale with whom I have a distant family relationship, which has always made me feel a special interest in her. In personality these two women were not at all alike, but there is a likeness in their capacity to accomplish an almost incredible amount of work in one lifetime and also in the way their influence pervaded a whole profession – in Susan's case all those who care for and educate young children and who train others for this work. Perhaps too there is a likeness in their deep human sympathy which prompted them to so much effort and the very wise and strategic, but nevertheless formidable, opposition they could put up to those who wilfully, or from mere apathy or conventionality, disregarded human interests and human needs.

In some respects Susan was a pioneer and, as such, encountered some opposition and even enmity, but to most people she appeared as a friend. Many pioneers, in their deep concern for a cause, lose sight of the individual; that was something Susan never did and for that reason she made few enemies. I of course am writing as a friend, and as such may be suspected of partiality. If so, I can only reply that the picture of Susan as I have tried to give it has been endorsed by many others who knew her well in her later years. Moreover, if my love for her had not remained safely 'this side idolatry' Susan would not have wanted me for a personal friend.

Whether or not she is remembered, her influence will live; but to forget the woman would be a loss to those who find inspiration in seeing great values expressed in a human life. I hope therefore this book will support those who wanted her to be remembered.

D. E. M. G.

*Contributors to this work to whom
I am much indebted for their generous help*

Those mentioned in the text are listed approximately in the order in which they occur in relation to various aspects of Susan Isaacs' life.

Mrs Alice Campbell (Susan's sister), Mr William Sutherland and Mrs Joan Maurer (cousins), Mrs Dorothy Rogerson, Professor Pear, Miss Elsie Shorter, Miss Naomi Clough, Sir Cyril Burt, Mr Joseph and Mrs Phoebe Pole, Lord Robbins, Dr Evelyn Lawrence (Mrs Nathan Isaacs), Mrs Margaret Pyke, Dr D. W. Winnicott, Mrs Len Chaloner, Dr Lois Munro, Dr Paula Heimann, Dr Jean MacFarlane, Mr Arnold Campbell, Miss Sybil Clement Brown, Mr George Lyward, Miss Mary Maw, Miss Margaret Metcalfe Smith, Miss Dorothy May, Dr Edna Oakshott Miss E. M. Ingram.

*Those not mentioned in the text who have also given
generous help*

Mrs Dorothy Glynn, Mr and Mrs A. J. Jenkinson, Dr C. E. Beeby, Miss Elaine Price, Miss Daphne Bell.

1 · Childhood

On the 24th of May 1885 a ninth child was born to William and
Miriam Fairhurst in the village of Bromley Cross near Bolton,
Lancashire. The child was baptized Susan Sutherland, the second
name was that of her mother's Scottish highland family. In later
life Susan loved the highlands of Scotland but also took great
pride in her father's Lancastrian ancestry, and since her childhood
and youth were spent in Lancashire she always thought of it as
'home'. Like all loyal Lancastrians and Yorkists, Susan would
immediately react with indignation if anyone implied that the
two counties were in any way alike and insisted firmly that
speech, traditions, and landscapes were in fact quite different,
though she bore no ill will to Yorkshire! Yet I am compelled
to admit that my first sight of her native village awoke in me
a wonder which many visitors to Haworth have expressed,
'Can so stark and sombre a background have produced such
genius?'

To Susan herself her native town and village and above all its
surrounding country were not only dear but in a sense also
beautiful. In a talk she gave in New Zealand entitled 'A childhood
in a Lancashire cotton town' she said: 'The streets of the town
were grey and grimy, with their long rows of slate-roofed cot-
tages, uniform in pattern, the doors opening straight on to the
street without a green leaf or a space between . . . yet there was
a certain dignity in the very bareness and stark simplicity of the
streets. They belonged to the bare moors with which they were
surrounded. . . . They clung together with a neighbourly warmth,
and their solid grey stone and slate, and stark lines, were not so
alien to the moorland heights, not such unworthy fellows to the

old manorial halls of the county, as their more sanitary successors of the twentieth century. From a hillside, it was of course the mills and their chimneys which dominated the landscape. The little houses clustered round these great square buildings whose tall chimneys pierced the smoke and mist, each belching out its own addition to the general grime. But what sunsets, what silvery light the smoke and fog would bring to those moorland views.' She adds: 'I returned to my home town a year or two ago, after an absence of many years. In the time between, I had seen many mountains and valleys, many lovely landscapes in other parts of England and the continent of Europe. And the brightness of these experiences had dimmed my memories of my native county – had led me to think of it always as of mills and chimneys, of grime and smoke, of machines and hurrying workers. I looked again on these – not so grimy now, not hurrying so fast. But I saw also that it *was* here that I first learnt what a good landscape was. I saw how noble those moors are, what grand open lines they show, what dignity and breadth their dark heather has. And as if for the first time I saw how pleasantly the valleys turn, how charmingly they are wooded, how much in keeping the little stone houses appear. I could think away all the modern outcrop of red brick, now spreading itself without regard to contour; I could see again the countryside as I knew it as a child – and see that it *was* good, in spite of the factory chimneys and the crowding streets of the towns, and that it *was* here that I first learnt to love noble hills and space and freedom.'

She spoke also with great sympathy and intimate knowledge of the lives of those who worked so hard and saved so strenuously. Although her father at the time of her birth had achieved moderate prosperity by his work as a journalist, this was only by unremitting effort and with the very able support of his wife who, with strict economy and very little, if any, domestic help, maintained very high standards in the home and in the care of her large family. By the time of her death, when Susan was six years old, William Fairhurst was editor of the *Bolton Journal and Guardian* and had been able to afford to build a good-sized house on the outskirts of the town, though his wife did not live long enough to move into it. This house, named Monksfield, was much loved by the family.

I once asked Susan whence she derived her tremendous energy and she unhesitatingly answered 'from my mother'. Her cousin William Fairhurst confirmed this and said that Mrs Fairhurst was remembered by many in the village as a woman who performed household tasks with speed and efficiency and sometimes did her ironing with a baby on her lap. Bessie, Susan's oldest sister, who knew her mother best, described her as 'a very dignified woman, not too tall, always immaculately dressed even at the very beginning of the day, calm of face, strong willed, rather aloof' and also as 'an exceptionally fine, intellectual, and helpful companion to her husband'. Her children undoubtedly loved her and Bessie, though only thirteen at the time of her mother's death, seemed always at hand to help her mother in the house or in nursing the babies. At a later stage it was Susan who helped Bessie and after Bessie's marriage stayed at home to assist with the household duties. There was nothing in the house that she could not accomplish with efficiency and speed, while still directing the main part of her energy to very different interests.

In these days it would have been quite out of tradition for the men to help in household affairs. Alice, the youngest daughter, records that on occasions when she and Susan disputed about whose turn it was to clear the table and wash up, her father would rise from the head of the table, look very severely at them and say slowly and majestically, 'I will clear the table.' She says, 'We would be so utterly appalled that no more would be said and we would for quite a long time take our turns properly.'

William Fairhurst, as well as being a journalist, was a Methodist lay preacher. He is remembered by those who knew him as a man of intellect and scholarship and, though severe in his standards both moral and intellectual, was a person of considerable charm who certainly inspired affection. Alice described him as 'that beloved man' and remembers instances of his kindness and sympathy, but also tells of being sentenced to a good many meals of bread and water even for such slight things as too frequent grammatical errors in her speech. Her father's concern with language no doubt influenced the whole family. To the end of her life Susan never failed to note, though seldom censoriously, any error in verbal expression however minor or commonly used it might be. She was much too courteous to subject children or students to what she had often suffered as a child – the humiliation of being required to repeat her remarks in correct grammatical form, but she would tactfully put a word or phrase right for students and was very critical of 'slovenliness' in the language of published and deliberate writings; her reviews of these could be severe. She had achieved the art of clarity and grace in speaking and writing, and in all her professional work she was able to help others to clarify their meaning and to find the right word or phrase.

From her earliest years Susan was surrounded by certain influences the effect of which can be seen in her later life, and as her biographer I regret that so few people remember, and in such scant detail, the personalities of her parents, brothers, and sisters.

Susan was the seventh surviving child in the family as two had died in infancy. I shall refer later to the influence of her three oldest brothers, Willie, Enoch, and Archie, and of the two sisters who came next to them in age, Bessie and Miriam (Mirrie); but the deepest very early influence probably came from the sudden death of the brother Harry, just above her in age, who developed pneumonia before Susan was eight months old. She was not to have long before influences caused by grief affected her life. She was still at the breast when Harry became dangerously ill and their mother, distracted by anxiety and exhausted by nursing the sick child, had to wean the baby Susan very suddenly and almost abandon her except for giving really essential attention to her physical needs. Harry died, and between this tragedy and the birth of Alice four years later Susan said she remembered some blissful hours when she had her mother to herself.

It is probable, however, that such times were not very frequent as Mrs Fairhurst was still fully preoccupied with household tasks and the care of her family, and there were troubles with two of the older boys. William, the oldest, left home to join the Mercantile Marines when Susan was under three years old. She was very much attached to him and so, from a child's point of view, it was very like another bereavement; her analysis later revealed that in fantasy she felt she had damaged and driven him away. He left home under a cloud of family disapproval and Susan was not at an age when she could take an objective enough view to free herself from personal involvement. How early it came to her that the great pleasure of her mother's undivided attention was gained at the cost of her (rival) brother's death, and just how the realization came to her, is a matter which I am not qualified to pronounce on, but that it did come and at a very early stage in her life was something of which she was later to be keenly aware and which exerted great influence on her.

A still more severe shock and grief came at the age of four when, after the birth of Alice, Mrs Fairhurst succumbed to an illness which lasted for two years and from which she never recovered. The household which had been so perfectly cared for gradually fell into disorder and discomfort, and Susan remembered sometimes playing not as a happy child plays, but as a desperate one trying to find comfort or at least distraction. At the age of five she was sent to the local infant school and welcomed this as an ordered place where they wanted her to learn.

She described her own motives for her great eagerness to learn as being 'I'll show them I can do something'. She also remembered a teacher whom she said she would have 'done anything to please' looking at her sewing and telling her to 'make her stitches smaller' and her own bewilderment as to how this could possibly be achieved since the stitches were already there and no further advice given.

Perhaps such experiences were the beginning of her deep conviction that learning is one of the ways in which we achieve stability and happiness, and that young children need to be taught in ways which they can understand. The desire to please is, of course, strong in all young children, but perhaps particularly so in a child who so much lacked the normal reassurances which come to children when their parents and brothers and sisters are not in fact destroyed or made ill by the young child's possessive love, his aggression when frustrated, and his wish to push out anyone who is between him and the person most desired at the time. All her life it was clear that Susan was deeply touched and really surprised by evidence that people loved her. In early life she seems to have found the experience almost overwhelming. Her determination to show people that she could do good things was, no doubt, part of the picture, and also her desire to make reparation for harm which in fantasy she had done. However, her passion for learning and overcoming obstacles very soon became established in its own right and in later life she was almost indifferent about pleasing people when it was a matter of the pursuit of truth. She was shocked by any suggestion that she should suppress evidence in order to avoid unpopularity and showed herself able to resist even those whom she most admired and most deeply loved when they urged her to change over from clinical work where she had much less status, but where she felt she could learn most, to the educational world in which she could have held a leading, even a unique, position and been much more appreciated. The desire to 'show them I can do (good) things' also freed itself from the need to 'show them' and gave way to her other prevailing passion, the desire to help people – which again she felt was more deeply achieved by remaining in clinical work. She sometimes spoke of 'my incurable weakness of wanting to be useful' which was very much stronger in her at the time I knew her than any wish for recognition. Indeed she was often careful to see that those she helped were not aware of the source from which the help came. She rejoiced when a patient had recovered and therefore did not need her any more and appeared to forget her, though she took the deepest possible pleasure when she heard news from other sources of his success. If I ever mentioned with gratitude any help I had received or seen others receive from her, she had usually forgotten that she had given it. Her vivid understanding of the reality of feelings in young children also I think owed something to her own early experiences of grief and was probably the most important influence of all. A letter to a friend who had asked her advice about a proposed book for children reveals something of her own memories of difficulties in her childhood. She wrote: 'I do not think I have any criticism; the only doubt perhaps being that so few little children will have such wonderfully considerate and understanding parents as those in the story and I wonder whether it will not make some little children rather wistful – I confess it had something of this effect on me. Perhaps it might not, however, on a tiny child, because for oneself it carries all the weight of misunderstanding and lack of consideration that one encounters in the world'.

Mrs Fairhurst's illness increased, unsatisfactory housekeepers came and went. It was clear that more help was needed and so a nurse was employed who also helped with household affairs. William Fairhurst gradually came to feel great affection for this nurse and married her not long after the death of his wife. Susan's last meeting with her mother was inexpressibly painful because a comment made by the six-year-old little girl revealed the growing affection between her father and the nurse. Her mother was too ill to bear it and demanded that Susan should ask God to forgive her for telling such a lie, which the child felt powerless to do when what she had said was in fact true. Then someone came into the room and took her away. She never saw her mother again. The memory of her mother's white face and anguished eyes remained with Susan all her life.

With her mother's death Susan's early childhood may be said to have ended, though she received much kindness from her eldest sister, Bessie. Susan always thought of Bessie as her 'mother–sister'. Miriam, the second daughter, mothered Alice, then aged two. Bessie was very critical of the apparent disloyalty to her mother of her father's rather speedy second marriage and she disliked her stepmother. This no doubt would influence Susan, and by all accounts the stepmother was not a very warm or sensitive person. Alice too appears to have disliked her though, being very young, perhaps less than the others. There was great affection between the brothers and sisters who knew each other, but two of the brothers had left home and Alice never remembered seeing the whole family together nor even two of her brothers at any one time. Susan did retain very affectionate memories of all her brothers, but Willie and Archie at that stage were, she said, 'very wild'. Archie ran away to join the Army and was definitely under the cloud of their father's strong disapproval, though both brothers later 'made good'. Willie was seldom at home. With Miriam, Susan's relationship was never as close as with her other sisters or with her brothers. She was very attached to Enoch, the steadier brother, who was more often at home and who became an artist, and she was also very fond of Alice. With Miriam there may have been more rivalry – she was lively in social situations, whereas Susan and Bessie were more shy and sensitive. Miriam later had a distinguished political career in South Africa. The whole family appear to have been gifted artistically as well as intellectually. Enoch was a 'cellist as well as an artist. Susan herself was very musical. Some friends of the family expected her to make her career in that field. The family, however, appears to have been regarded in the neighbourhood as distinctly 'Bohemian'. Susan said they were left without any social training and though she maintained that her stepmother did try to do her best for them in a very difficult situation, there is no doubt that in some ways they did not experience the care and guidance which would have been theirs if their mother had lived. Susan remembered at the age of six being sent off alone to the dentist to have a tooth extracted and afterwards running sobbing over the railway bridge aware that she had missed the train home.

Another of her six-year-old memories was of leaving her home to go to the house of an old friend of the family's who had sometimes asked her playfully if she would like to be his little wife one day. Having fallen into trouble at home she arrived on his doorstep and said she had come to marry him now. He took her in and gave her a kindly welcome, dispatching a message to her home. They sent back a parcel with a message that if she was going to be married she would need clothes, but when she opened the parcel it was filled with newspapers. She then realized that she was an object of mockery and went home deeply humiliated. Her vivid memories of the sensitivity of childhood were to be used again and again in the way she advised parents and teachers to explain things to children, or on how to handle difficulties in their upbringing.

Her awareness of how conflicting the feelings of children can be also developed very early in her life because, in loyalty to her much loved sister Bessie, she withdrew from her stepmother and could not allow herself to show affection for her. She would really have liked to have her stepmother's love and felt some identification with her because of her own love for her father.

Alice's letters give some vivid pictures of the family life at that period. She writes, 'It must be remembered that Ma had been a nurse in some of the toughest wards in different big city hospitals, and all her adult life had been disciplining really hard cases, and she was at a loss in her handling of my beloved sister [Susan] . . . I clearly remember the day on which we moved into the house, and an incident on that day which, although I was only a little over two, impressed itself on my childish mind. It throws an early light on the relationship between our stepmother and Susie.

'Bessie pushed my little child's carriage with me in it along the lane to the house, with Sue walking beside me, and of course when we reached the house she and I began to investigate the garden. In the backyard was a drain with one of those removable grids and Sue, to whom it was new, let her foot go down one side and into the drain, and Ma just laughed and laughed. I can still see the hurt, puzzled expression on Sue's face, an expression I was to see very often from time to time, and it must have been something quite incomprehensible to Sue; her memories of Mother and her instinctive knowledge of what Mother would

23

have done at the mishap, compared with Ma's attitude, must have immediately raised a barrier between Sue and our stepmother.

'To those who loved Sue and understood her sensitive nature I think this little incident must appear very significant. However, there we were, in the new house.

'Sue and I shared a big bedroom at the back of the house, just at the top of the stairs – a good strategic position for creeping out to watch the activities of our elders, and listen to their conversation.

'Sue was always the ringleader in our mischief and I a willing follower of one with an eternally inventive mind.

'Until the new Secondary School was opened in Bolton when she was twelve, Sue went to a Council School, memories of which were always very bitter to her. The year after she commenced at the new school, I too became a pupil there. We travelled to and from school (home to midday dinner) by the local train, and it was in the frequent train journeys together that we got into endless mischief.

'Father was a very staunch supporter of his chapel, and Sue and I had the dreariest of Sundays. We commenced each one by attendance at morning Sunday School, then on to Chapel Service, home to the heavy English roast beef – Yorkshire pudding dinner, back to Sunday School, home to tea, early Prayer Meeting, evening Chapel and then some other Meeting to round off the day. It could be a Prayer Meeting, a testimony meeting, or a "love-feast" at which sacrament was administered.

'I think the testimony meetings really gave us the greatest pleasure, because Sue and I always knew what to expect in advance. There was one woman with her husband sitting alongside, who would time and again repeat the same exhortation to the Lord to bring her husband to "see the Light". She would kneel with the pew seat in front of her, thump it with great thumps, and say "Lord, make him miserable, until he sees the Light!" And it was well known that the poor man was the most harmless of creatures. Father always finished the meeting by the most dignified of prayers, which apparently affected Ma so much that she would gently weep. Sue and I would watch through the fingers over our eyes and try to control our giggles.

'We were always abominably dressed – children often were in those days, with always our "best" tight laced-up boots and frocks with ghastly high collars. There again Sue was much more affected by the hideous dresses than I was. She used to plead with Ma for something more attractive, and as she grew older and was in a school class containing boys as well as girls, her distress became acute when Ma would not let her have longer frocks, and she became an object of derision to the boys. Where I would merely start a fight, she would suffer in dignified silence.

'This dignity of Sue's was remarkable. It was she who taught me very early not to fly into a temper, a lesson which has I think, stood me in good stead in later years. That ability to suffer indignities in silence exasperated our stepmother.'

Alice and Susan were often in trouble with their stepmother. Alice records many occasions when they were punished for their shortcomings by being given bread and water instead of their meals and refers to it as 'this miserable deprivation of our good food'. She adds: 'However, there was always plenty in the larder, and under Sue's direction when no one was looking, I would go down and raid the pantry to fill our ever-hungry stomachs. There again, our Victorian father simply did not see what was going on outside his all-consuming occupation as a very hard-working journalist. I well remember one incident when I had particularly annoyed Ma in some childish naughtiness – she said I would have nothing but bread and water until I apologized for my behaviour.

'I went to school hungry the first day (winter too), then Father did look at me and say "What is the matter with the child?" Ma explained my supposedly frightful behaviour to him and his only reply was, "Well, you cannot let her go to school on an empty stomach, so keep her at home." So home I stayed, until on the fourth day a visitor saw me and was aghast at my condition, whereupon Ma for the first time really looked at me and became troubled at her punishment. Again she tried to make me say I was sorry but my only reply was, "You'd be sorry to be hungry." Whereupon she produced a very lavish dinner and Sue really angered me by saying, "Oh when you have been starving it is dangerous to eat much at first. Please go slowly, or you will be ill."

'But not all our lives were unhappy; there was much pleasure also. Apart from the endless procession of services on Sundays, there was a good deal of enjoyable activity in connection with the Sunday School. Mirrie, the sister older than Sue, arranged many concerts at the School and of course we two children were always in the concerts. Mirrie was a very thrilling big sister to two youngsters, and seemed always to be the leader in whatever was afoot.

'I well remember one bitterly cold but brilliantly starlit New Year's Eve we were returning over the snowy fields from the Watchnight Service at Chapel, Father and Ma and we four girls. Mirrie made up and sang a little doggerel,

"The Fairhursts came home two by two,
Mirrie and Alice, Bessie and Sue,
Father and Ma brought up the rear,
And *that's* the way we do up here!"

'Sue had a very pleasing voice and tried hard to persuade Father to let her take singing lessons, but to no avail. Poor lass, she always seemed to be frustrated somehow.'

Like Susan, Alice also had charitable feelings for her step-mother as well as critical ones. She says, 'Looking back over the years I have come to realize that although the eldest of the children resented Ma, as we always called her, and quite naturally so – after Mother, she really did a very difficult job better than many other women would have done and looked after Father's indifferent health to an astonishing degree.' She also mentioned her as a very good hostess to her husband's many friends and says, 'Surely no one could ever have been ashamed of her. She quite wisely ministered to the physical needs with good food

26

beautifully prepared and arranged, leaving the conversation to the others.'

Alice several times refers to Susan's 'constantly inquiring mind'. She also mentions the many books and journals which filled their home and were eagerly read, and the high level of discussion both in the family circle and when friends came in and in which the children, when they were older, were able to participate. There was much fine music on some of these evenings.

The four girls all loved the countryside and explored the moorlands and all the surrounding country.

Susan writes: 'Turton Towers was older than Elizabeth, set in a wooded valley some miles from the town, and a romantic beautiful place to a child. It was a mystic delight to climb round and round up the steep stone stairs of the towers. And yet it never seemed quite real to me – not so real as the busy mills and the hurrying clogs. It was a dream, a story out of the books, set down in the midst of the countryside – a countryside which really belonged to the factories and the tall chimneys and the belching smoke, the coal mines and the never-ceasing looms.

'No, not altogether and only to them. For there were bluebells in the woods, wild white bird cherry and golden kingcups by the river in spring, in spite of the bleaching works on its course. There were the silver leaves of the white-beam on the hill, the heavenly scent of hay and the soothing sound of the scythe and cutting machine, in the summer. "The early pipe of half-awakened birds" called me out at dawn, to walk through the dew down the valley and come home with arms full of sweet bluebells and red campion. It was in Lancashire that I first learnt to love the blackbird and the thrush and saw my first pair of yellow wagtails. And it was here that I first learnt to love the line of the hills, and to judge a landscape from its contours on the map.'

It is clear, therefore, that despite much experience of early sorrow and many difficulties there was much pleasure too, perhaps especially in Susan's later childhood, and she undoubtedly

27

experienced warmth of affection from her sister Bessie. She was also very deeply attached to her father and had a great admiration for him. It probably accounts for her pleasure in writing, and she said it was her desire to emulate his preaching which led to her enjoyment later of lecturing. As a child she would mount the garden box or roller and deliver fiery sermons to the cabbages or any other suitable symbols of an attentive congregation. She decided she would like to be a missionary, and when she and Alice could secure an empty railway carriage on their journeys between school and home she would persuade Alice to kneel on the floor with closed eyes and hands together while she copied the revivalist preachers of the day by delivering sermons. Alice comments, 'Surely no preacher ever outdid this would-be evangelist in fervour.' Had the journey not been a short one, Alice would no doubt have rebelled. They were quite capable of having battles and certainly by that stage Alice could have held her own, but as the two youngest, often excluded from the affairs of the older members of the family, they were in close partnership and the affection between them persisted throughout Susan's life. Alice has no record at all of being bullied by a sister who was four years her senior.

Susan certainly had a reputation for 'naughtiness' at school as well as at home. A Bolton friend said, 'My word! She *was* a naughty girl at school – she used to play in class and the teacher would pounce on her and ask her questions, but she always knew the answers.' Susan remembered feeling real disappointment that a teacher whom she much admired was not able to manage her. She would at that period have described herself as a defiant and rebellious child. In later adolescence and early womanhood she described herself as over serious, and ascribed her later sense of humour and gaiety of spirit entirely to her analysis; but the memories of those who knew her in early life are of a child who could be both mischievous and gay though sometimes also very serious, and so it is possible that the analysis released again qualities which had been submerged by further troubles in adolescence. It seems, however, from the evidence

of many people, that she was never without a sense of humour
and, however rarely it might appear, a capacity for sparkle
and fun when life allowed her to relax. These qualities were
certainly characteristic of her in her later life, but even then
were probably revealed most often to close friends in informal
situations.

2 · Adolescence and Youth

It was to be expected that for Susan whose predominant characteristic, described by Alice, was that of 'a constantly inquiring mind', adolescence would awaken many new interests, enthusiasms, rebellions, and desires also for much wider exploration of the interests already firmly planted in her childhood. Her sources of knowledge were in and around her home, with its many books, highly intelligent older members of her family, and many intellectually distinguished friends of her father. School does not seem to have played very much part in her real education though, at the age of twelve, she had been able to leave the Council School which she disliked so much and attend the newly opened Bolton Secondary School where she doubtless found more scope to use what was quite clearly a brilliant intelligence. She was, I think, less critical of this school and was certainly regretful when forced to leave it. Her life-long concern with education was probably partly at least due to experiences of frustration when schools failed to meet her needs – together with some hope, derived from certain good experiences both in the Infant School and the Secondary School, that it was possible schools might, with more understanding teachers, become very different and deeply satisfying. Her brother Enoch was often at home and had a considerable influence on her growing mind. He introduced her to philosophical writings, and under his influence she became agnostic. This caused the next great sorrow in her life as it led to a complete rift with her much loved father. He was quite unable to tolerate his daughter's repudiation of his most deeply held convictions and for about two years refused even to speak to her. Her suffering was intense though she was never repudiated by Bessie. Indeed Bessie herself, probably a little later, identified herself with the same views. Miriam, I think, took sides with her father. Susan was removed from school though still under fifteen, her father's attitude being, 'If education makes women Godless, they are better without it.' She lived at home and helped Bessie and her stepmother with the household work. Of course she continued to read voraciously. Miriam and Alice were allowed to stay on at school and later both went to colleges to train as teachers. Miriam afterwards went to South Africa and married. The life-long very close tie between Susan and her eldest sister was, no doubt, cemented at this period. Alice writes, 'The one member never to go abroad or depart from the even routine of a household was the eldest of the four girls, Bessie, but what a lovable unselfish woman she was – so unselfish that she could never put *her* interests first. But they were there too, ambitions never to be fulfilled. In her spare time, and not too much of that, this sister wrote voluminously on two oddly contrasting characters, Charlotte Brontë and Napoleon.' An old friend, Mrs Rogerson, who knew the family at that time gives a clear picture of the home life of the two sisters. 'Their home was full of books of all kinds. Drawing-room, dining-room and bedrooms were lined with bookcases and Bessie and Susan were keen readers. They bore the chief burden of the housekeeping for years and their reward was five shillings each per week, out of which they had to dress themselves and pay for their amusements. They made their own clothes and in order to have time for study they rose at 4 a.m. Their kitchen was spotless, gleaming with brass. They reminded me of the Brontë sisters – they were great admirers of the Brontës and George Eliot. They used to come to our house, especially on a Sunday evening after service, drink coffee and eat toasted teacakes, and with other young people, discuss every subject under the sun in lively fashion.

'I remember Darwin's *Origin of Species* being very fully discussed. They had very strong ideas about women's suffrage, but I don't think either would have gone so far as to break

31

windows – they were too gentle – but they were great admirers of Mrs Pankhurst and Mrs Despard. They were full of ideas for social reform and declared themselves socialists, vegetarians, unitarians, and finally agnostics, to the horror of their father. They wore arty dresses of sage green which fascinated us. We always wondered what they were going to do next.

'In summer we used to go for whole day tramps over the moors – armed with baskets laden with delicious sandwiches of brown bread, dates, bananas, tomatoes and lettuce, walking round Entwistle, or to Rivington or Holdcombe Hill – there were no buses – and how we talked! They used to go to the Lake District for holidays, staying in a farmhouse in Patterdale.'

It was at this time that Susan very understandably developed what she herself described as 'over-seriousness'. Photographs of her in adolescence and still as a young woman show a very grave and often tragic expression. The characteristic sparkle and humour of her later life did not, it seems, appear at all frequently at this time. In her emotional development she appears to have matured rather late, and a very close friend of her girlhood and early womanhood says she never indulged in flirtations. If she loved it was with intense seriousness. If anyone loved her she was almost bewildered by it. She told me that once when she was a young woman and a man proposed to her she asked Bessie whether she loved him or not and when Bessie said 'No, you don't' she refused him! He was not one to whom she had been particularly attracted and the necessity of consulting her sister showed that where affection was involved she could not bring her acute and critical intelligence to bear on so vital a problem. Her father's repudiation, and possibly also anxieties related to her older brothers, may explain why in later life her deep affection was always given to men younger than herself. She told me that in adolescence she had once idealized a boy friend and was 'heartbroken' when he utterly shattered her illusions by writing her a letter which began, 'Hoping this finds you well as it leaves me at present' and she realized that she could no longer love him! Her first serious romantic attachment was, however, to her younger cousin Willie Sutherland and probably this was not till adolescence was quite past. Her main preoccupations in adolescence appear to have been her very keen intellectual interests and social contacts with a wide circle of friends of her own and her family's. She took part in dramatic performances, discussion groups, and concerts where she played the piano. She was also athletic and interested in sport but though she played games such as cricket, her main enthusiasm was for walking and climbing, a passion which remained with her through life. She had a remarkable degree of toughness and endurance and could out-last Alice though she too was a great walker and loved climbing. All four sisters used to tramp the moors and preferred hill country, rejoicing in the fresh landscapes revealed as they surmounted the hills. They were not daunted but rather exhilarated by the challenge of difficult climbing and rough country. (In later days Susan climbed mountains in Switzerland.) They passed through a phase of enthusiastic vegetarianism and outraged the conventions of the day by discarding corsets and all aids to feminine beauty. Once Susan and Alice set out on a week's tramping holiday provided only with packs of nuts, cheese, and dried fruit and became so hungry after their strenuous open-air life that they could not resist the attractions of a generous meal of ham and eggs provided by a kindly hostess in a farm where they spent a night. They were much ashamed of this lapse but decided eventually that they really needed a more varied diet.

Susan's reading ranged very widely in many fields though as yet the two which were to be her greatest interest later, psychology and education, were not among them. She began to read now and loved all her life, as her husband Nathan Isaacs said, 'the great European as well as English novels, and the whole world of poetry, from the earliest writers to the present day, but with a place apart in her mind for Shakespeare's Sonnets'. She also always loved music. Nathan said, 'Beethoven and

C

Mozart and Bach above all, but Sibelius almost as much, and then Schubert and Brahms and practically all classical music.' She always found deep pleasure in playing the piano.

Her reading included biography and history, and she became deeply interested in philosophy in which she later took her first degree. At this early stage she was greatly influenced by Paine's writings and Winwood Reade's *Martyrdom of Man* as well as by the more serious essayists like Emerson and Hazlitt. Whether at that stage she began reading biology, as she certainly did later under the influence of William Brierley, I do not know, but it became a very strong interest early in her adult life, and geology too fascinated her. She had for a long time been studying these subjects through first-hand investigation; later she became an ardent bird watcher and was able to detect the presence of any hidden bird by recognizing its song. Flowers too were an endless source of delight and interest to her and she enjoyed searching for rare ones.

Her quick human sympathies led to an early and deep interest in politics. She was keenly aware of the struggles and often acute poverty of those who worked in the mills. She writes: 'When the six o'clock hooters go, the dark valley will be starred with thousands of bright squares of light from those factory windows. The men and women, weavers and spinners, piecers and little piecers, foreman and hands, will be hurrying into these grim cold noisy buildings. . . . The stone steps are worn hollow in the middle with the constant tread of the clogs, six times daily up and down the stairs. How those clogs echo in the grey stone streets, typifying the hard unchanging grind of life in those grey industrial towns. At six o'clock and eight o'clock in the morning, at half past eight and half past twelve, at half past one and at half past five, you can hear the rhythmic clatter of iron upon stone. The shawls and clogs which hurried through the streets, to and from work, six times a day, were thrown aside on Sundays. The gayest and smartest of clothes were worn for church and chapel and Sunday school – women's forms and faces emerging like bright butterflies from the cocoon; but unlike the butterfly, returning again to the closely gathered shawl on Monday mornings, when the machinery began to whir once more. For one week, and one week only, in the year's round, were the looms and spinning mills, the coal-mines and warehouses, left altogether behind. Each of the great industrial towns, Bolton and Preston, Chorley and Oldham, Wigan and Blackburn, had in its turn its one orgy, its *wakes*, its week of freedom and fun and high gaiety at Blackpool, where the money earned so hardly and grimly was flung gloriously away. Times were not always prosperous, even in the nineties and early nineteen hundreds. I remember periods of pinching and even of famine among the cotton workers. . . . There was no unemployment benefit, no insurance, no general social responsibility for starving children, and skilled men could not find work. But fellow feeling was strong and direct . . . the chapel or the church called upon the lucky ones in half-time, if not in full-time, work to pool their resources for the more needy. Many families who attended the Wesleyan Chapel in my own village deprived themselves for a week or a month of all butter on their bread or sugar in their tea and paid the savings into the common fund for the help of their less fortunate friends.'

Alice records that when Susan was sixteen and she twelve there was a disastrous strike in the cotton mills and the consequent near starvation of the people was appalling. 'Sue decided to help as far as she was able (we never had pocket money) and persuaded me to do without butter for months, if Ma would give us the money saved towards the rebel fund. So for quite a long time we willingly ate our bread dry. And why, you may well ask, did such a way of raising a little money in a good cause occur to us. Surely it was the biggest sacrifice we could make, bearing in mind the hardships (to hungry children) that we had so often been forced to bear in the form of dry bread and water, whilst watching the rest of the family partaking of the really appetizing dishes Ma used to produce.

'Sue and I bravely denied ourselves until the strike was over, although we had to put up with a good deal of sarcasm and amusement from some of the chapel folk who could never give the Fairhurst girls credit in the right place.'

Susan's ardent interest in socialism at that period sprang from her humanity and sympathy. In later life the interest in politics was one of the few which she discarded in favour of other channels for her abiding desire to help people. Nathan Isaacs writes, 'As from the early twenties onwards her focus of interest became more and more psychological and above all psycho-analytic. She withdrew her interest from the field of practical politics and her socialism, though never abandoned, became more and more a mere background, part of a general philosophy of humanism, freedom and justice.' While still living at home she joined the Fabian Society and also became an ardent though not militant supporter of the Women's Suffrage Movement. Later, at Manchester University, with Clifford Allen and others, she became one of the founders of the University Socialist Federation.

Except for a short period after leaving school when she was apprenticed to a photographer and found this work unsatisfying, Susan may be said to have been conducting her own education, while still being responsible for much of the housework. Naturally she gave some thought to the question of what she wanted to do, and eventually decided that she wanted to be a teacher. She took a private post teaching a young and delicate boy. At that time she had no hope of her father's consenting to her going to college, but later she obtained a post with an English family who wanted to employ a nursery governess to go out to Morocco with them for a year. I have not been able to trace the exact date of this appointment, nor did she ever talk about it to me. I believe she was quite happy and enjoyed the opportunity of horse-riding.

After her return she taught again for a time in a small private school in Bolton but, realizing how handicapped she was for lack of training, she managed to persuade her father to allow her to go to Manchester University to take a training which was then available to non-graduates who wished to become qualified infant school teachers. Her father permitted this because he felt that young children were, after all, the province of women! He had already allowed two other daughters to train as teachers and his repudiation of Susan was probably by then gradually weakening. After Bessie left home on her marriage, which I think occurred about this time, Susan and her father became reconciled. But the question of finance was still likely to be an obstacle. Bessie was critical of her father for spending as she considered extravagantly on himself while they, like her mother before her, had to exercise strict economy – which they did very conscientiously.

At the time Susan took the course at Manchester she was considerably older than most of her fellow students, probably twenty-two or twenty-three. The Head of the course was Grace Owen who was already well known as a pioneer of progressive education for young children. She inspired Susan with deep interest in the writings of Froebel and Dewey. Susan was quick to appreciate Miss Owen's knowledge and wisdom and longed for further discussion with her; so being, as she afterwards said, quite untrained in social etiquette she asked Miss Owen if she might come to tea with her one Saturday. Miss Owen's response was cordial and Susan stayed on in ardent discussion till late in the evening. When, in later years, she apologized for this, Miss Owen replied that she had enjoyed it and had not wished her to leave a moment earlier. Indeed, Miss Owen was so aware of Susan's quite unusual intelligence that she spoke to Professor Findlay, the University Professor of Education, and said she felt that Susan should leave her course at the end of the first year and be encouraged to take a degree. He therefore sent for Susan and put the proposition to her. Susan, to her great embarrassment, was unable to control her tears. She seems to have received sympathetic treatment and was able to recover herself and explain how much she longed for this chance of further study but how convinced she was that her father would oppose it. Though she was of age, his financial support would be necessary as she was entirely dependent on him. Professor Findlay said he would write to her father, and very fortunately the fact that his daughter's outstanding intelligence had won the notice of so eminent a professor aroused his family pride and pleasure so that he gave his consent. Susan was able to obtain a grant dependent on a pledge to teach, which helped with the expenses, and he supplemented this with a small allowance. Even so, she had a struggle to manage on the money. It was a case of sandwich lunches and walking rather than taking buses.

The greatest struggle, however, was to surmount the academic hurdles between her and eligibility to enter for a degree course. She had left school before she was fifteen and had no qualifications. Two foreign languages were part of the essential requirements, and it was then that her cousin William Sutherland coached her in German. He said he was aware that the whole family were hard workers, especially Bessie and Susan, but he was amazed at the capacity for intense effort Susan revealed at this time. She learned the Greek and German necessary for university entrance in three months, and although he helped her with German idioms, colloquializations, and pronunciation, she did the rest herself. He was deeply impressed. At that time she gave him an overwhelming impression of a very earnest student with a 'terrific' power of concentration and a tremendous determination to make up for leaving school so young. He said she was determined to study and win knowledge but that the later direction of her life was not yet determined. It appears, therefore, that she had already begun to have doubts about her wish to teach. This doubt eventually grew stronger and led her, when circumstances permitted it, to repay her grant and so leave herself free to choose another career if she wished.

William Sutherland describes her as like Bessie, 'very much a Sutherland with the characteristics of the family, a pronounced nose, small and stocky, tough and wiry'. This description does not suggest beauty but by many Susan was judged beautiful. She had the rather rare combination of very fair curling hair and exceedingly bright brown eyes, her mouth was sensitive and flexible, and her chin strong so that the rather pronounced nose did not throw the face out of balance. She had too the charm of a musical speaking voice, though William Sutherland did not consider her rather small singing voice particularly engaging. He admired her piano playing. He was undoubtedly attracted by her and she very much, at some stage, by him. Indeed at one time they both looked into the question of whether marriage between cousins was desirable, and though in the end the idea of marriage did not persist they were always good friends. But after 1911 they seldom had the chance of meeting though they continued to correspond. Possibly Susan was at that time a little intellectually awe-inspiring to him, fond of her as he undoubtedly was. He describes her as having no small talk, but says she would chatter away unrestrainedly to him and adds that she was 'essentially serious, but had her own kind of humour'. And she had other interests besides her passion for study. She enjoyed parties in cheap seats in the gallery or pit of the Gaiety Theatre where the performances were never second rate. She was interested in sport and would often come to watch him play hockey. And there were social week-ends in which she joined groups of interested people got together by his father where there was much talk and much determination to 'put the world to rights'. In a letter to me after a meeting when we had talked together about Susan, he wrote: 'I greatly enjoyed our two talks. You and I knew Susie in such widely differing circumstances that at first we seemed to be talking about two different people, but then it became clear that the struggling and very hard-up student and the scholar with an established reputation were indeed the same person, with the same tenacity of purpose and fine personal qualities.'

At last the academic requirements were satisfied and Susan was able to enter the University. But her enjoyment of this achievement after all her effort and longing was dimmed by the death of her father which occurred during her first year. Susan certainly assisted her stepmother in nursing him through his last illness; whether this interrupted her studies or took place in the long vacation I do not know. Susan had for six months been living with a friend so that she could be nearer the University and Alice was the daughter who was living with her father for his last six months. She was then aged twenty and Susan was twenty-four. Susan experienced very great distress in attending her father during his illness. He died of a perforated ulcer, which doctors say would not have killed him now; Susan believed that with greater care it need not have occurred, though Alice was convinced that his wife at any rate had looked after him well, and she herself was devoted to him.

William Fairhurst left no will and the proceeds of his estate, which was not large, were divided between his widow and daughters. The three sons gave up all claim, which again illustrates the good feeling between the brothers and sisters. It was this small legacy which enabled Susan to repay her grant and manage by strict exercise of economy to pay her own way through University.

3 · Maturity

At twenty-five Susan was studying intensely at Manchester University. As before in her childhood, the opportunity to learn was a solace in her mourning for a father who, despite the bitter period of estrangement, she nevertheless deeply loved. She read philosophy under the famous Professor Samuel Alexander and quickly won his interest and respect. Mrs Rogerson, who was then a fellow student, writes: 'I always used to think that Professor Alexander looked like a very kindly father when he talked to Susie. Miss Sheavyn too thought very highly of her.'

Professor Pear, another of her University teachers, remembers her as a brilliant student with an original mind. He said that in those days it was rather usual for students, especially the women students, to demonstrate their intellectual independence by arguing for the sake of arguing, but that Susan never did this. She was very sensible and had her feet firmly planted on the ground, but her mind was like the early type of wireless apparatus known as a 'super heterodyne set' which could take messages from anywhere. And while so great a diversity of ideas would distract and confuse some people, she remained serene and able to take and assimilate them all. He found her quick to appreciate the impact of various kinds of knowledge on any situation – for example, her swift realization that the findings of some of Piaget's early work would be limited by the way in which the evidence was obtained and the whole setting in which the work was done. Professor Pear commented also on her exact and vivid use of language – 'she could have been an excellent journalist'. He later showed some of her writings to Professor Myers and told him of her wish to study more psychology; after the briefest glance through her papers, Myers said, 'Let her come to Cambridge and I will see she gets a scholarship.'

Susan made many friends among her fellow students who admired and very much liked her. Much later when one of them, Miss Ellen Wilkinson, became Minister of Education and I had to go on a deputation to see her, Susan asked me to give her a personal message of good will and congratulations. I stayed behind after the official business and delivered this message. Miss Wilkinson looked blank until I said 'She says you will remember her as Susan Fairhurst,' whereat she said with keen interest, '*Not* Susie Fairhurst? Is *she* Susan Isaacs? Of course I remember her. She was our star student.'

At Manchester Susan was elected as president of the women students. Mrs Rogerson, who had known her in earlier days and said that her family always remembered the four sisters with admiration and affection, writes: 'Susie was always kind to me when I was a child, and later at Manchester took me under her wing and made my years at the University much fuller than they would have been without her. She was quite the most outstanding woman student of our time. My first year coincided with her last year. She went to live with Nan Griffiths, another philosophy student. She continued to make all her own clothes and brought sandwiches for lunch. Her circle of friends included the most brilliant students in the University, men and women, but she, Nan Griffiths and I used to eat our sandwich lunch together very often. She sailed victoriously through all her examinations, ending with a First Class Honours in Philosophy and a graduate scholarship with which she went to Cambridge to study under Professor Myers. . . . She was always a keen student but never a mouldy bookworm. She was not beautiful in the accepted sense, but had beautiful fair curly hair, fine teeth and a lovely smile. She had beautiful manners always and great charm.'

One of her friends was William Brierley, then an outstanding student of Botany. He later used to visit Susan and a friend with whom she then lived; Susan believed at first that he was attracted by her friend but afterwards discovered that it was herself;

whether they became engaged at that stage or later I do not know, but he was continuing with his studies at Manchester when she went to Cambridge.

Her mind was gradually turning from philosophy to psychology and she very much welcomed the award of the scholarship in order to take up the study of psychology. But I understand that her philosophy thesis is still cherished at Manchester as a shining example of what a first thesis in the subject can be. There is no doubt that the background of clear and rigorous thinking from the study of philosophy contributed to her later work, although as Nathan Isaacs said, 'Her interests soon underwent a further evolution which turned her more and more away from the generalities and abstractions of philosophy to the concrete and living field of psychology and the possibilities of knowledge-increasing research.'

Life at Newnham was very different from that at Manchester and to Susan it felt rather like entering a young ladies' seminary. She recalled with amusement that she was not even allowed to receive her brothers without the presence of someone in the capacity of chaperone! She did not, however, appear to be particularly irritated by this. The opportunity for further study eclipsed for her any minor irritation and, as always, she did not lack friends. Nor did she seem to mind that, as was customary, her tutor chose her research subject for her and put her on to investigating the causes of good and bad spelling. He thought she might find evidence that good spelling went along with good visual perception, but she was not able to find this evidence and said that the only thing she did find was a tendency for good or bad spelling to run in certain families. To those who knew her later it has sometimes seemed a matter for regret that she was not assigned to something of greater human interest, but she herself had no regrets. She threw herself whole-heartedly into the quest, worked as always with tremendous energy and drive, and said she learnt much of the disciplines of research. She later published a report of the inquiry. She also made full use of the opportunity to study general psychology. The emphasis then was on

43

experimental psychology, and medical and child psychology, which included the work of Binet and Janet. One day while she was working in the psychological laboratory, she noticed a visitor examining a calculating machine and, as she thought he appeared puzzled, offered to explain its use. He led her on, enjoying her explanations, and she later discovered that he was the already famous Cyril Burt! She was not a little indignant that he had encouraged her, as she felt, to make a fool of herself.

Though her period of study at Cambridge was only one year, she had by the end of it come to the fore as a research student of distinction and one with unusual insight into psychology. Professor Myers thought very highly of her. Her M.A. was a residential Cambridge one. Her D.Sc. was conferred later for her publications, particularly her book *Intellectual Growth in Young Children*.

Even at this early stage in her study of psychology, Susan's attention was turning sharply to children. Her cousin's daughter (now Mrs Joan Maurer) describes how Susan, sometimes accompanied by William Brierley when she was in Manchester, though still working in term-time at Cambridge, would come to see her mother and give advice and help about the child. She writes: 'Susan was intensely interested in my development and helped my mother with suggestions about small furniture, a tea service of my own, creative materials, and a form of control which was based on reason rather than authority. Willie, however, tried very hard to ignore me and to make Susan do the same, but there was one occasion when I had been given Plasticine so that he would not notice me and I made a pansy with every detail of the back of the flower carefully represented and his botanist's heart momentarily melted with enthusiasm.'

When she left Cambridge Susan was appointed lecturer in Infant School education to Darlington Training College. Miss Freda Hawtrey was then Principal there and when I asked her what Susan was like at that stage she said immediately, 'beautiful and gifted'. She described her to another friend as having the most outstanding intelligence of any person she knew. She also told me that Susan was much in advance of her time in her educational ideas. I have been fortunate in having some evidence from two of the students who worked with her then, one of whom, Miss Elsie Shorter, got to know her very well later. She writes: 'Her lectures were outstandingly vital and stimulating. Her work was always thorough, and she made her students attack their work with the same thoroughness and stimulation. No student willingly missed one of her tutorials though perhaps we went up to her room with a slight feeling of dread – her criticisms were severe and searching, but never unjust or scathing. Her aim seemed always to make her students think and analyse and criticize for themselves. Moreover, she had a knack of ending the discussion on a constructive note and finding for each one of us some good point in our favour so that we left feeling stimulated. Amongst the other lecturers she held her own in argument and discussion and was well respected and liked.'

Miss Shorter heard later that some action on her final teaching practice inspection evoked much criticism and argument at the high table that evening but – 'Miss Fairhurst defended me so convincingly that I gained my distinction.'

The other student, Miss Naomi Clough, said that she felt at that stage Susan did not reveal her personality: 'She was immersed in her search for the true methods of teaching. One student, however, found contact with her. She was Miss Shorter. She was like Miss Fairhurst in her impersonal attitude towards others and quite dedicated to her work. . . . I was a student from 1913–16 and fortunate indeed to have her tuition in Education and Psychology. In both these subjects her ideas were very advanced, giving us exciting glimpses of "things to come". We also had tutorials when groups of students were introduced to the fascinating facts of Embryology and were shown specimens in bottles! We learnt, through experience, how "projects bring knowledge to the children in a practical and interesting way, as well as giving them the joy of creative activity". The group of students with which I was working, were asked to make a "house" their centre of interest! Two of us were given the

45

bathroom to furnish. My partner asked me if I thought her wash basin was big enough. I said, "I think it is too big," and was reprimanded by Miss Fairhurst for speaking.

'It seemed curious that, in spite of her vision of a new freedom for the children, she was quite strict with students. It may have been a precaution against too much excitement on the part of the emancipated students, for, being used to the formal methods in schools, we were indeed very thrilled by the new ideas. Her attitude to students in general was rather remote.'

It is possible that lack of experience with students partly explained the episode described by Miss Clough about Susan's refusal to let the students talk when planning their work – I cannot imagine it would have happened at a later stage in her teaching life. Miss Clough's short account also reveals what Susan herself later laughed about – the fact that in her passion for thoroughness she made her first students study much biology as a necessary preliminary to the study of psychology. Miss Clough, however, seems on the whole appreciative and her point of view probably represents that of the general attitude of the students to Susan's teaching.

It was during her year at Darlington that Susan and William Brierley decided to marry, and when both Susan and Miss Shorter were about to leave they became friends rather than tutor and student.

Miss Shorter relates that they talked about 'everything under the sun, including wedding arrangements and her new home and husband. The wedding was, of course, in a registry office, the wedding "dress" a tramping outfit – heavy boots, rucksacks, etc., and the honeymoon was spent tramping the hills. She loved the simple life and simple things and beauty. I stayed several times at her new home in Levenshulme and my liveliest memory is of getting up early on a Sunday morning, taking a train to somewhere in the Peak district, tramping all day and coming home at night to a whopping big meal, then winding up sitting lazily round a big fire.'

Miss Shorter decided after leaving college to take further

qualifying examinations and Susan offered to coach her, which she did with characteristic thoroughness, recommending many books and lending them, reading her essays, and answering her questions. Miss Shorter records: 'I wrote regularly on topics of her choosing, the criticism was as always severe – often almost devastating, but by a later post would be a kindly letter telling me where and how much my work had improved and suggesting lines of development. She never seemed too tired or too busy to do this for me. . . . All my immature ponderings on religion and life after death and many such subjects never aroused her impatience or ridicule but she could always find time to answer as fully as possible.'

At that stage in her life Susan was prepared to go to any pains to prevent a friend, for whom she clearly cared deeply, from basing her religious convictions upon what seemed to be not evidence and she wrote long letters gently but firmly disposing of arguments which seemed to her unconvincing. In later life she avoided discussion of issues on which her views might, she felt, upset people's religious convictions. In both cases her respect for the personality of others was paramount and in her long letters to Miss Shorter it was clear that she felt it was a service to clear away delusions. Two short extracts will perhaps show her attitude: 'Why oh why if the blessed freed souls really wish to give us proofs of immortality, do they not do it properly and convincingly? Why is it all so vague, so full of surmise, so accidental and so trivial and paltry? One can only think they leave their intelligence behind with their bodies or they would find some really useful way of proving their existence after death.' . . . 'My dear, it's a little cruel to suggest that I want to "explain away" anything. I only want to find the solid truth as distinct from mere subjective belief and cloudy surmise. . . . Should you *want* to believe either way in particular? Surely you should want to get as near the truth as you can, but you mustn't first think what you would *like* to believe, and then try to find supporting reasons for this view. Our effort should be to discount personal desires although I agree it is very hard to do so.'

47

The University of Manchester offered Susan an appointment as a lecturer in logic in the philosophy department. She held this appointment for only one year because at the end of that time William Brierley obtained an appointment in research into plant diseases at Kew and they came south and lived in a top flat looking over Richmond Park. About a year after their removal Miss Shorter came to teach in London and records:

'The flat was beautifully furnished with simplicity and good taste. Mrs Brierley introduced me to the fabrics of Liberty's and curtains, carpets, bedspreads all came from there. She was a good housekeeper and cook and everything was marvellously organized and running smoothly. Once again her delight in simple things and in the outdoors was manifest. She loved to wander in Richmond Park and many a Sunday morning we spent in Kew Gardens. It was not open to the public but her husband being on the staff had a key and we would sit in a quiet corner and feed the squirrels. These always knew that our pockets would contain nuts for them. Once again evenings always consisted of a pleasant meal followed by a firelight session. One typical re- mark of hers: I had been appointed to an East End school and she took me to find it. I was appalled – a narrow grimy street, a four storey building – high spiked gates, dirt-encrusted windows protected by iron grilles. Mrs Brierley saw my face drop and took hold of my arm and said quietly, "Never mind, my dear, look up. There's always the sky," a philosophy that has carried me through many a difficult place in my life.

'Another London memory. She took a discussion group – W.E.A. I think – in a room along the Edgware Road: the subject 'Psychology and Life'. One of the students was an old rag and bone man, long dirty beard, matted hair, dirty old coat often tied round with string, but his eyes were alert, his face had a twinkle, and his contributions to the discussion were un- usual and intelligent. Mrs Brierley was most intrigued. We would walk to the tube together after the class, still discussing him.

'Another London thought. I was a young teacher and very badly paid and finding it difficult to make ends meet. At the time

I had a free invitation to the Richmond flat but that invitation became very definite – the last week-end in every month. She never referred to my lack of funds for that special week-end but made very certain I was fed. For me a lasting memory of great kindness and friendship.'

Susan not only lectured, as Miss Shorter records, for the W.E.A. but was also enrolled very soon after her arrival in London as a lecturer for University Tutorial classes. These were busy years. By 1921 she had published her *Introduction to Psychology* with its very marked biological approach, and had for some time been turning her attention more and more to Freudian psycho-analysis and the flood of new light which she felt that this study threw upon the deeper and more obscure life of the mind. She had already started upon her first long analysis with Flugel in order to learn what this new discipline had to teach. Her sphere of activity continued to spread.

She became associated with the work of the National Institute of Industrial Psychology and was appointed a member of its council. She also took a keen interest in the British Psychological Society and served on its editorial board from 1921 for many years, indeed for most of the rest of her life. Sir Cyril Burt recalls papers she gave at meetings of the Society, and she had published articles before the appearance of her first book.

It was gradually becoming apparent both to Susan and to William Brierley that the marriage they had entered upon with intense seriousness was not proving wholly satisfying to either – William Sutherland, when talking about the engagement, said that William Brierley was more than Susan's equal in seriousness and that at the time of their marriage Susan was deeply impressed with the seriousness of love and completely idealized William Brierley. He also referred to her total lack of early experience in flirtations, which may explain why she was possibly liable to over-idealistic feelings, or it may be that the developing personalities and interests of both gradually drew them further apart. Both were intensely loyal to each other and I should doubt if even their most intimate friends were told of any difficulties.

When Susan realized that she was beginning to feel a deep affection for Nathan Isaacs she deliberately avoided all meetings with him for two years and then came to realize that William Brierley too might find greater happiness if she left him.

The marriage was ultimately dissolved, and Susan married Nathan Isaacs in 1922. She expected that this would cause her to lose some of her work and many of her friends. Her appointment with the W.E.A. was certainly terminated. She stopped corresponding with friends to whom she felt contact with her might now be an embarrassment, and that included Elsie Shorter (who ultimately guessed the reason for it) and many years later the friendship was renewed. William Brierley also re-married, a younger friend of Susan's, and very friendly relations between all four people were re-established.

Before joining Nathan, Susan went abroad for a time and had a short analysis with Otto Rank, but this was merely to deepen her insights in a study which had been engaging her interest for a long period. There were rumours that this analysis had been the cause of her separation from William Brierley, but that was quite untrue. Nathan Isaacs joined her in Germany for a holiday before they set up their home together in London.

There was no mistake at all about the second marriage. They met first when Lionel Robbins (now Lord Robbins), who had been a friend of Nathan's since they met during the 1914–18 war, brought Nathan to attend Susan's tutorial classes in psychology held at Bell Street in the Edgware Road. Two other friends of Nathan's, Mr and Mrs Pole, also persuaded him that these classes would be of great interest to him. Indeed, the Poles attended for the full three or four years of the course, which Lord Robbins was unable to do for more than two terms. He said it gave him academic relief from his work in politics, and Nathan was equally thankful for such relief from the world of financial business. Lord Robbins remembered that Susan's lectures were 'very well composed'. Each lecture was followed by an hour of discussion. Nathan very soon became the main questioner and 'they were at it hammer and tongs'. He describes Susan as very poised, rather prim, and very clear and lucid, with never an obscure sentence, whereas he said 'Nathan could get lost in a flurry of words'. The Poles said that Susan was quickly taken by Nathan's intelligence and much impressed by a long essay he wrote for her on the body and the mind. They describe him at that stage as having an inquiring mind, a great zest for life, and very considerable charm, and said: 'Susan admired these qualities. He wanted to explore and she was always willing to explore, but as yet his intelligence was untrained and Susan felt motherly.'

Nathan was ten years her junior in age. Lord Robbins says Susan gave him what a university education might have given him. Both also participated in week-end discussion groups arranged for university people. Susan had a great admiration for Lord Robbins and from the time she first met him in 1919 she too became a friend of his. Knowing them both so well, Lord Robbins gives an interesting and perceptive account of the way in which Susan and Nathan influenced and helped each other then and also in later life. He says: 'Nathan was an introvert, living in an inner world. Susie was essentially a realist, very firmly down-to-earth and with a much more systematic mind, empirical, crystallized and systematically arranged. . . . Her "Now Nathan" got him down to earth. He helped her by criticism and argument to look more closely at matters where he felt her psychology was not adequate. He lifted her out of any attitudes which might have become conventional. Her own career might have been less without him. . . . He was a big man to live with . . . [but Susan's] influence made Nathan the impressive person he became. Unless he was in actual contact with reality he became unreal. . . . Susie was intensely aware of the people she was talking to – Nathan lived in a world of concepts rather than direct sensation and was not particularly sensitive to the effects he was producing on people. He was really tender hearted, it was just that it didn't connect up, whereas Susie had spiritual antennae waving all round her head.

. . . Nathan came to psychology from metaphysics and his brooding about the nature of the world. Susie would not have

woven large metaphysical schemes and had long since given up
the idea that you could find one secret to explain everything.
Nathan had terrific psychological energy which must have been
very stimulating to live with. He was fortunate that in his
marriage, and also in his second marriage after Susan's death, he
had a woman at his side who made him intelligible and effective.'

Susan firmly believed that his intelligence was superior to hers.

Susan and Nathan were married in 1922. Susan was still in
analysis with Flugel and began to take a medical training, as she
wished to become a medical psycho-analyst. She passed her preliminary examinations, but did not proceed further and go on to
the wards because she decided that it would be hard on Nathan
financially if she did not help by her own earning. He was not
aware of her reason for dropping the medical training but at her
request he had bought a house in Bloomsbury. She felt she should
not have asked for this and did not want to increase his expenses
any further. She was by then sufficiently qualified to take patients
for analysis. She was elected to full membership of the British
Psycho-Analytic Society in 1923, having already been an Associ-
ate Member for two years. Professor Flugel gave me his memories
of her at the time she was in analysis with him and described her
character as generous and sincere. To him and also to her second
analyst, Joan Reviere, I owe many of the factual details of her
childhood, as well as to Susan herself. Professor Flugel said at
the time he knew her that she was much concerned with the idea
of separation, and that these anxieties related to the loss of her
mother after Alice's birth. He referred to an incident she mentioned when an ardent socialist who had called at her newly
furnished home said of the curtains and cushions she had made,
'Of course, all these things will have to go.' He condemned them
as plutocratic luxuries and she said: 'Do I really have to be parted
from these poor little things I've made myself?' Flugel said it
was characteristic of her at that stage to have thought of the
incident in terms of separation. No analyst, of course, would
reveal anything of a confidential nature about a patient, and it is
merely my own surmise, supported by what Susan herself once

52

said to another friend, which leads me to think that, though in later years she very much wished that she had had children, the anxieties about possible loss of life may have played a part earlier and explained why, though it was quite true that neither William Brierley nor Nathan Isaacs had wished to have children, she herself did not confess her wish to either husband. Nathan, like Susan, was very fond of children (not merely the theoretical 'child') but he suffered from the deep pessimism which affected so many of his race after the 1914–18 war and made him doubt whether it was right or fair deliberately to bring children into a world such as this. Susan herself once confided her feelings to a friend who had children of her own, and who writes: 'When the youngest child [in the Fairhurst family] arrived the mother became invalided and this made a deep impression on the little Susan. It made having a baby seem terribly dangerous to the little girl who at the same time longed to grow up and have babies of her own. I gathered that this conflict of anxiety helped to interest her in analysis. But even in spite of her great love for children and her close links with her nephews, she said she could not really overcome the deep-laid childhood fear until she was too old wisely to start. So in her own way the intense longing became transformed and she had thousands of children through the help she gave them almost all over the world from her work. Her love for and understanding of children is born out like a thread woven through all her work and way of life, and it is hard to imagine any child who would not come to love and trust her.'

4 · Fulfilment

(i) The Malting House School

To some extent Susan's life until this point may be said to have been a long and thorough preparation for the two greatest contributions of her life which came from her work first at the Malting House School and later at the Department of Child Development. She was already deeply concerned with education before she went to the Malting House School and continued to be so after she relinquished her appointment as Head of the Department of Child Development at the University of London Institute of Education, and it is probably with those two achievements that she will always be specially associated. It was certainly her work at the Malting House School which arrested the attention of the educational world and caused her work to be known by those who had not previously heard of her.

In the spring of 1924 a startling advertisement appeared in display type and edged with a striking border which occupied a whole page in certain journals, including the *New Statesman* and the *British Journal of Psychology*. The advertisement, which was reproduced in full by Dr Rickman in his obituary article on Susan Isaacs, read:

'WANTED – an Educated Young Woman with honours degree – preferably first class – or the equivalent, to conduct education of a small group of children aged $2\frac{1}{2}$–7, as a piece of scientific work and research.

'Previous educational experience is not considered a bar, but the advertisers hope to get in touch with a university graduate – or someone of equivalent intellectual standing –

who has hitherto considered themselves too good for teaching and who has probably already engaged in another occupation.

'A LIBERAL SALARY – liberal as compared with research work or teaching – will be paid to a suitable applicant who will live out, have fixed hours and opportunities for a pleasant independent existence. An assistant will be provided if the work increases.

'They wish to obtain the services of someone with certain personal qualifications for the work and a scientific attitude of mind towards it. Hence a training in any of the natural sciences is a distinct advantage.

'Preference will be given to those who do not hold any form of religious belief but this is not by itself considered to be a substitute for other qualifications.

'The applicant chosen would be required to undergo a course of preliminary training, 6–8 months in London, in part at any rate the expenses of this being paid by the advertisers.

'Communications are invited to Box No. 1.'

Dr Rickman comments that on reading this extraordinary statement one's curiosity was divided between speculation about the personality of the advertisers and that of the individual bold enough to answer it. Susan's first reaction was to assume the advertiser to be a crank, and when Nathan suggested she should reply to it she was at first reluctant to do so. However, he prevailed upon her – with the result that the author of the advertisement, Geoffrey Pyke, and his wife, and Susan and Nathan met for a series of discussions of the project and, when this had revealed a very considerable measure of agreement in their ideas, Susan consented to take on the task of conducting the school. Geoffrey Pyke agreed that she was to have full responsibility for this and described her function as being equivalent to that of Prime Minister and his own to that of the Crown in a democratic country.

Dr Rickman writes: 'Pyke was a man of untrammelled imagination. Whereas with most people the movement of the mind is somewhat constrained by the habit of centuries and the custom of the multitude, with Pyke these facts neither slowed and constrained nor reactively stimulated the flow of his thoughts. To mention but one typical venture of his mind, during the Second World War when Atlantic sinkings were considerable and the defence of convoys difficult, he it was who suggested unsinkable islands of ice and sawdust (kept from melting by enormous diesel-powered refrigerators) cruising slowly far out in the Western Approaches: such imagination and engineering insight is rare – it was typical of his sweeping grasp and bold planning. His teeming brain conjured up many such projects.

> I may thank my fortune for it,
>> My ventures are not in one bottom trusted,
>> Nor to one place; nor is my whole estate
>> Upon the fortune of this present year.'

But not so Susan Isaacs. What had she to lose by undertaking this piece of educational research? Her career had followed an academic tradition. . . . With such a career behind her she took a venture in an experiment which ignored convention and challenged nearly every prejudice. It was characteristic of Susan Isaacs to take the risk of such an enterprise, to sober down the extravagance of her fellow-workers, and by great common sense and intellectual grasp of the essential issues to lead the venture to novel, practical, and constructive projects – and finally achievements. When the school's prospectus was finally printed, it contained an imposing Advisory Board – the advertisement was by then forgotten. It is here brought to light again to show Susan Isaacs' skill in leadership: an extravagant idea was turned into a sober plan of action.

After about two years Evelyn Lawrence was appointed to the staff. She gives an account of the early planning and aims of the school. She writes: 'Pyke had both critical penetration and vision of a high order. One of his particular gifts was to uncover in the social system around us some of the major stupidities, muddles, and inefficiencies which the rest of us take for granted, and to suggest practicable remedies. Or at least the remedies were

56

practicable provided that they were not blocked by the recalcitrance and the wilful blindness of the human beings concerned in them. One of the things Pyke wanted to change was the education of young children. He had some valuable general ideas about the matter, some practical schemes, and the means to finance them. He persuaded Susan Isaacs to plan and run a small school in Cambridge where new ideas would really be tried out.

'Though the school was essentially Susan Isaacs' creation, other minds were at work on those early plans. Pyke brought to the symposium a keen dissatisfaction with education as it was, flashes of penetrating theoretical insight, and a great deal of practical ingenuity. Nathan Isaacs brought years of philosophical and psychological thought directed particularly to the meaning of knowledge, the processes of its growth, and the relationship between thought and the instrument of language. Susan Isaacs herself brought from her early training as a teacher and her later university work in philosophy, logic, and psychology, the essentials of an intense concern with education, a deep knowledge of and sympathy with the most advanced educational thought, and the new illumination provided by psycho-analysis. In many discussions before the school began they tried to put aside the acustomed ways of envisaging education and to think the thing through again from the start, though naturally their thinking was greatly influenced by that of earlier pioneers, particularly Dewey.'[1]

It seems valuable, at the risk of slight repetition, to give both Evelyn Lawrence's appraisal of the main features of the school when looking back on it and also her contemporary impressions of it. At the time of Susan's death in 1948 she wrote:

'Probably the three most interesting contributions of the Malting House were the attention paid to the child's spontaneous

[1] Tribute should also be paid here to Margaret Pyke's invaluable contribution to the success of the school. She shared her husband's ideas and vision, and placed her own capacity and energy unstintingly at the service of the school. Her part in the practical work of getting it going and coping with its manifold problems was certainly no less than that of others.

urge towards finding out, to all the influence on his thought exercised by and through language, and to his emotional needs.

'It was felt that one of the chief educational aims on the intellectual side was to give the children the best possible start in the matter of clear thinking and independent judgment.

'Each generation by its general ways of thought and its confused and careless use of language passes on some of its own muddles to the next. At the Malting House the children's thinking would be watched and every attempt made to keep it straight as it went along. And adult responses to the children would also be watched so that confused habits of thought would not be passed on. Opportunities were taken of letting the children observe that the grown-ups often differed from one another in tastes and opinions; and rules and prohibitions were deliberately relaxed on occasion so that they should not appear to be unalterable laws, but should be seen to be man-made and capable of being influenced and reconsidered. The body of adult attitudes, opinions, and preferences would thus be shown to be susceptible to change and development, whereas the world of scientific fact was something to be accepted and necessarily adapted to. Perhaps this all seems to be not a matter for babes, and, of course, explicitly it was not: but the attempt was to create a mental climate which would be favourable for the right kind of mental growth. The essential point, as Dr Isaacs saw it, was that if you did not get these things right with the babes, you would never get them right later on.

'Another very important aspect of the intellectual part of the educational problem was to foster in every possible way the children's joy in discovery. Here again, they were studied individually, and when one of them put out an intellectual feeler an attempt was made to ensure that the feeler met the kind of situation which would encourage it to go on. The primary logical stages of the main divisions of learning – mathematics, language, biology, history – were borne in mind all the time, and the physical environment and the adult behaviour so arranged that the children were naturally led to notice, to explore and to follow up. To give one small illustration, the see-saw had weights which would hang on at intervals below the beam, so that the children might spontaneously observe the physical effects of the different distributions of weight about a fulcrum.

'On the emotional side, Dr Isaacs was guided from the outset by the new insight into behaviour contributed by psycho-analysis. Very little accurate observation of young children in groups had been recorded, even on the level of their conscious behaviour, and it was very necessary that a fresh start should be made in the light of a fuller understanding of the influence of their phantasy life, and of the roles played by love and hate, by aggression and guilt. If the children were to be really observed they must be freer than a normal school group would be allowed to be. The force of the feelings which the conventional would consider disreputable could never be estimated, nor the child helped to deal with them, if no expression of them was ever allowed. There was, therefore, no nipping in the bud of every hostile act, every sexual interest, every bit of dirtiness or rebel-lion. The art of the educator is to learn to judge the right place for drawing the line in these matters. It may be doubted whether any school could ever allow complete freedom or enforce complete control. Dr Isaacs was trying to get more light on what the balance should be, to find a valid theoretical basis for future practice, to bring some order into the knock-about of disciplin-arians versus libertarians.'

Susan Isaacs' own description of the school is given at the beginning of her book *Intellectual Growth in Young Children* and her findings are contained both in this book and in its companion volume *Social Development of Young Children*.

Evelyn Lawrence has also given me permission to quote in full the account of the school as it appeared to her shortly after joining the staff. She writes: 'The following account of the Malting House School was written in 1927, when it had been running for two and a half years. The document was not intended for publication, but was produced in response to an invitation from Dr Isaacs to set out my first impressions, when I had been a member of the staff for only a few months. A few minor alterations have been made, but it is substantially as it was written at the time. It does not pretend to be an adequate description, but it has the merit of being contemporary with the school, and it may help to answer some of the questions which are often asked.

'The purpose behind the school seems to me to be twofold. In the first place there is a definite group of children to be educated. Something has to be done with them. They cannot be put back to sleep until educational theory has devised the perfect method of bringing up the young. Such psychological and pedagogic knowledge as has been arrived at can, however, be used for their benefit, and this is being done. The lag of practice behind principle which characterizes most schools was seen to be avoidable, and is here being avoided.

'But principle still has very far to go. The child psychologist has not yet completely formulated, much less solved, his problems. One of the reasons for this is that, under the old coercive methods of education, it was almost impossible for adults to know the minds of children. A few parents or teachers may have known their children well, but the number with both the inclination and the psychological training to describe them scientifically is lamentably small. It was felt, therefore, that an indispensable preliminary to improvement in educational theory was a detailed and consistent study of a group of children living under conditions of the maximum freedom. This study is being made, and at the same time innovations in educational practice are being made and tried out.

'For the practical educator, there are again two problems. To begin with, however much he may want his human plants to flower freely, and nature to take its course, however much he wants to break bad precedents and keep his new generation away from the shadow of the past, he knows that many courses are open to him, and that his choice will probably affect the whole lives of his pupils. He must therefore decide what kind of people he would like to produce. Secondly, having made this decision, he must find out how to get the desired result.

'The kind of people that the promoters of this school want to produce will have a scientific attitude to life. They must have intellectual curiosity and vigour, and be averse to taking their opinions ready-made. They must also be as physically healthy as is possible. I think this is as far as Dr Isaacs would go in particularization.[1] She is anxious that the decision as to what exactly the children should become should arise naturally from the children's own characters, aptitudes, and inclinations. Capacity for successful adjustment in society is included in the scientific attitude. Social ability is largely an intellectual thing, and if we can create reasonable people a large part, at least, of their social battle is won.

'The emotional life of the children makes an even more difficult problem. Our chief concern is to produce a new generation less nerve-ridden than the old. The newest psychology has taught us something about what to avoid in the way of repression, what kind of attachments should be encouraged and what discouraged, what sort of emotional outlets should be provided. This knowledge is being acted upon as far as possible, and new light looked for from the observation of this group of children.

'I will come to what is actually done in the school. The best way to prepare a person for life is to safeguard his zest for life. The Malting House children certainly have it. When I first came to the school I tried to decide what was the most striking difference between this school and any other I have known. I came to the conclusion that it is the happiness of the children. Not that I have not been in happy schools. But I have never seen so much pleased concentration, so many shrieks and gurgles and jumpings for joy as here. Of course this joy is particularly apparent because its expression is not hindered. If you want to dance with excitement you may. But even if the contrast is made with a free home environment the distinction remains.

'I suppose the reason for this happiness is that there is plenty

[1] For her later views on adult maturity, see Appendix I.

of space, that material equipment is abundant and suitable, and that the child is free to use it in ways that appeal to him, instead of being forced to do with it those things which his elders consider good for him. It is delightful to be in a school where the usual answer to the question "May we do so-an-so?" is "Yes," instead of the almost automatic "No" one finds oneself expecting.

'The consequence of this policy is that many activities which all children love, but which are usually indulged in when the Olympians are safely out of the way, go on in the school under the full eye of Olympus. These children play with water and with fire, they climb and swing and even smoke, with the grown-ups not indulgently turning a blind eye, but approving and helping. As a result these games are robbed of the fictitious charm usually given them by the need for conspiracy, and those in which this was the only support die out. For example, D. has a pipe of his own, but does not smoke it. Activities such as climbing and playing with fire, which contain an element of danger, are carried on in the presence of older people who can make sure that accidents do not occur.

'I will describe the school briefly. There is a large schoolroom opening into the garden. At one end of the schoolroom is a platform with a piano, and at the other a rest gallery with mattresses, pillows and rugs. Round the walls, below the window, are shelves and cupboards holding the material which the children use. This is very abundant. There are things for drawing and painting, sewing and modelling, brightly coloured raffia, canvas and wools; the Montessori-material; material for counting, such as counters, beads and shells; an aquarium, a gramophone, books and glasses and bowls for bulbs. Each child has a small table and chair which it can carry about. These have been painted by the children themselves in gay colours. A swing hangs from the gallery.

'Beyond the schoolroom is a cloakroom with bowls for washing, and a gas stove where the children make their own cocoa, and occasionally cook lunch.

'In the garden are an open summer house, a sand pit, a see-saw and hutches for the rabbits. Each child has a plot, and there are fruit trees whose fruit is gathered, cooked, and eaten by the children.

'As well as the large schoolroom there are two small rooms where the older children spend part of each morning. Here the more advanced number and reading material is kept, and apparatus, such as dissecting instruments and test-tubes, glass vessels and burners, for scientific observation in zoology, chemistry, and physics. A carpenter's bench, a lathe, and a quantity of tools have recently arrived, and one of these rooms will probably become a workshop.

'Leading from these schoolrooms are the children's bed-sitting rooms. Each child living in the school has one to himself. These rooms are charming. Each is painted in some bright colour, and each has a gas fire and a settee bed, gay curtains and cushions, and low tables and cupboards. In his own room the child is absolute master. The doors will lock from the inside, and no one is allowed to enter without knocking.

'The school is designed primarily for very young children. All those now coming are between the ages of three and seven, with the exception of one ten-year-old. Several are the children of dons and all are above average in intelligence.

'There is no fixed curriculum. The children do what appeals to them at the moment. The work of the educator is so to select his material, and at times indirectly to suggest activities, that the child will of his own accord do things which are useful for his growth. Lately one or two of the older children have drawn up rough outlines of their day's work. The categories are very wide – for instance, part of the day is devoted to "making things and finding things out" – and their order was arranged by the children themselves after discussion with the Principal. No child would be forced to keep to his programme if he seriously wanted to depart from it at any time.

'The older children voluntarily spend part of each morning at reading and number work. They have reached the stage where they feel the need of reading and writing, and are learning rapidly with no urging. They find the number material interesting and like to use it, though the most valuable part of their number training is probably incidental. A good deal of time is spent in "finding things out" with the help of gas and water, glass vessels and tubes, simple mechanical apparatus, skeletons, and animals alive and dead. A rabbit, crabs, a mouse, and worms have already been dissected. Textbooks will be home-made, in the form of written records of what has been observed.

'The younger children spend a good deal of their time in running about, in conversation, and in simple handiwork. No work involving fine hand or eye muscles is encouraged, and no attempt is made to teach them to read. There is, with all the children, much more active movement than one finds in most schools. In fine weather they are out in the garden for most of the day, digging, running, carpentering, or climbing. Even when they are in school the door is often, and the windows always, open. They are encouraged to swing from bars, jump, and supply for themselves in play the kind of exercise which in most schools has been elaborately worked out as drill and gymnastics. The consequence is that their health is excellent. There has been practically no illness since the school began. In two instances people were actually in the school with infectious complaints, which no one caught.

'The aim of the teachers is as far as possible to refrain from teaching, but to let the children find out all they can for themselves. They are urged to answer their own questions, with the teachers to help them discover where the answers are to be found. Above all, care is taken that their ideas of values shall be their own. They are not told that such and such a thing is good or bad, nice or beautiful, but only that it seems so to some particular person.

'Discipline is very free. There is no punishment, and little admonition. Prohibitions, when unavoidable, are of particular acts, not of whole classes of conduct. It is not true, however, that the school is entirely without rules. It is generally understood

64

that material used shall afterwards be put away. If the user (as often happens) is reluctant to clear up at once after his game, he is allowed to wait until he feels more inclined. But the matter is not forgotten, and sooner or later he usually agrees to put back what he has used in its place. Another rule is that implements must not be used as weapons. If this happens, the weapon is gently but firmly taken away. No anger, however, is ever shown by the teacher. If the two participants in a serious quarrel are unevenly matched, there is intervention on behalf of the one who is at a disadvantage, so that the weaker child does feel that he can get just support.

'There are three main advantages of freedom of action and emotional expression. In the first place you can get to know your children. Under the old disciplinary methods the educator knew his pupils only very partially and mistakenly. The child was forced to wear a mask of seemliness and respectability in the presence of grown-ups, and behind that mask his own inner life bubbled unseen. Here the children's crudities, the disorder of their emotions, their savagery even, are allowed to show. Emotional troubles can then be dealt with scientifically, or allowed to straighten themselves out, as they so often do, given time.

'Secondly, the danger of driving strong emotions underground, to work havoc in the unconscious, is avoided. The open expression of sexual interests is allowed, but where possible they are canalized by being turned into scientific channels. This freedom entails a certain amount of unpleasantness for the grown-ups. It is useless to expect children to be free at times, and at others to exercise discretion in situations where discretion is usual. But one cannot have it all ways, and it is time conventional parents learnt that their children are not the little angels they had believed. Hostility, another uncomfortable passion, is allowed freedom of expression. If the Malting House children hate a person, they tell him so. It is then possible to investigate the reason for that hatred, and probably to remove it. Fights and squabbles often occur, and if the fighters are fairly evenly matched, they are left to work out the adjustment themselves.

'This leads me to the third advantage of freedom. With conventional discipline, the child is kept wriggling under a dead weight of adult disapproval and prohibition. Here his position is that of a fencer, continually adapting himself to the shifting conditions of the group mood. This is what he will have to do in adult life, and it is surely a mistake to make all his social adjustments for him until adolescence, then pitchfork him into the world to discover from the beginning how human relationships work. When you have fought with another person over a thing, you realize that his desires are as strong as your own, and also, eventually, that fighting is not the best method of settling differences. The result of this policy in the school is not anarchy. I have seen several children combine to prevent conduct which they rightly considered unjust, and I have seen children of the most forcible character voluntarily submit to the leadership of a weaker-natured child.

'The position of teacher in such a school as this is not an easy one. He needs patience, self-control, and a great deal of alertness. He must be able to see the implications of the children's remarks, questions, and acts, and respond appropriately with no appearance of indecision.

'The second main function of the school, that of providing source material in the field of child psychology, entails the keeping of detailed notes. The children are under trained observation out of school hours as well as in them. In fact, there is no break between their school and their out-of-school life. Practically all that they do, and much of what they say, is recorded. The children are discussed individually, and the meaning of their actions, as well as how to deal with them, considered. Very much valuable material has already been accumulated.'

'Looking back after a space of over twenty years at this description of the school, I should record that at the time I was not without doubts about the possible effects on the children's future

66

manners and habits of the degree of freedom which they were allowed. Furthermore, was there enough positive attempt to help them to build up attitudes of kindliness, unselfishness, sensitiveness to the things which remain unexpressed but which are important in other people's lives? Were they going to see the value of giving more than a *quid pro quo* in personal relationships?

'Time has shown that I need not have worried. When the Malting House School ceased to exist a number of them went on to other schools working on free methods. Others went to more formal schools. In neither case was there difficulty in adapting to a new environment, and in establishing satisfactory relationships with their schoolfellows and teachers. We have remained in touch with a number of them, and they have developed into young men and women with pleasant and easy manners, and with an adequate sense of social responsibility.'

As was to be expected, changes took place as Susan viewed the developing situations with her keen and critical mind. She was always generous to the ideas of others and gave full scope to trying out ideas which seemed to justify experiment, but if they failed she was swift in her awareness of the fact. Two ideas of Pyke's which, for example, she found necessary to modify were that *every* question should be referred back to the child, and that children should never be told the name of anything but rather asked 'Shall we call it so and so?' Children were sometimes exasperated by this referring back of questions and said 'If I knew, I shouldn't have asked you, should I?' Also it confused them not to be told the accepted name for any object, and it seemed hardly sincere to make it appear to be a matter of children's individual choice. Pyke was concerned that children should be taught to realize that language was a convention and that words were not objects, but Susan became convinced that young children could not be given that idea in this way and probably not at all till a later stage in their development.

Another change was made after a visit by Melanie Klein. Until then, although the children had been restrained from using physical aggression, verbal aggression had not been checked, but Susan's own doubts as to whether this was not sometimes too painful to be tolerated by the victim and productive also of guilt in the aggressor were reinforced by Mrs Klein's views. Evelyn Lawrence states: 'During the life of the school Dr Isaacs' own position changed somewhat. As a result of her observation of this group of children, and of the discoveries of Melanie Klein which were then first becoming available, she realized increasingly the young child's need for order and stability, for adult support of his loving and constructive impulses against his own hate and aggression; in short, for an element of guiding firmness. Nevertheless, the final conclusion was that children can and should be allowed much more freedom of speech, of movement, of enterprise, of interest and of experiment than most schools give them.'

The school attracted many visitors, among them Professor Jean Piaget who was deeply interested in the evidence it afforded that very young children can sometimes reason in a logical and realistic way in situations where they are personally involved and deeply interested. He later paid generous tribute to Susan's work and said it had led him to use fresh techniques in his own investigations. Though at that stage of his work Susan challenged some of his conclusions, there was also a considerable amount of agreement and she very often quoted his findings with great respect. I think it may be said that even in Piaget's earliest studies she would agree that what he claimed to be true of the thinking of young children did apply in many situations, for example, where questions were asked of children or thinking was required of them by others, but that their intellectual powers were sometimes released at a higher level, especially in situations of spontaneous investigations through their play. She was very conscious that children were not at one level all the time and mentioned an incident that the same child who had aroused Piaget's interest by giving a completely realistic account of how a tricycle worked, on another occasion when angry because a kettle spat at him, spat back at the kettle. She would have agreed,

I think, that Piaget had shown teachers the most that can be expected of young children in test situations or when receiving formal teaching. She was, of course, also aware that the Malting House children were very intelligent, but though she would have admitted that they would therefore reveal higher levels of thought more often than less intelligent ones would do, she would have held that it was a question of 'more or less' not 'all or none' and that the thinking of all young children was closely allied to motivation and genuine interest.

Critics of the school were, of course, not lacking. The idea of giving so much freedom to young children alarmed the conventional, and extraordinary stories about it were circulated in Cambridge. Susan kept a collection of them and was interested to trace the original sources of rumours which grew into something quite untrue. In one case a child had broken his collar bone during a party held in the Christmas holidays, but later the story arose that he had done it in the school because she had refused to help him climb down from a tree. One rumour, of which she was never able to trace the origin, was that when a new child did not want to come into the school she had allowed him to sit in a taxi all the morning with the fares ticking up and had sent the bill to the parents!

She was serene in the face of unjustifiable criticism and also ready to disclaim exaggerated statements from well wishers of the miracles she was sometimes presumed to have worked.

Dr Rickman describes how she was asked to attend a learned discussion society in Cambridge of scientists and those interested in psycho-analysis, to give an account of the school and what a memorable occasion it was for the society. He believed, however, that she had been hurt by one of the criticisms expressed, but Nathan said that was not so. It would not have been characteristic of her to resent scientific challenge to her work and Nathan could not have been unaware of it if she had been so hurt that, as Rickman said, she would never accept another invitation; she would certainly have gone again if asked to do so.

Rickman himself was keenly aware of the value of the school both to the children themselves and to our knowledge of young children. He mentions particularly the contribution it made to our understanding of the nature and function of fantasy and play. He writes: 'Play, as Susan Isaacs wrote after her experience at this school, "is the child's means of living and of understanding life". . . . One has to cast the mind back twenty-five years to realize that this was then a bold if not (in the teaching world) a revolutionary notion. It was revolutionary not only among educationalists, but even among analysts, for at that time some would have regarded play as the embodiment of an unstable shifting imagery of unconscious erotic impulses and not "a means of living and understanding life". The school endeavoured to give the child opportunity for imaginative play, free and un-hampered by adult limits and teachings, and it recognized (as few teachers then did – or do now) that the child's own body is used for imaginative play since the child, owing to its im-maturity and inexperience, has as yet so little skill in subordinat-ing materials. Teachers may for their own understanding draw distinctions between fantasy and experience, and momentarily separate them, but the young child does not, and because the young child does not, the research workers in the fields of education must plan their technique of observation accordingly. As these notions are too general for a research programme the matter was made more specific by regarding the master key to the child's development as the solving of problems, problems of skill, of seeing and understanding, of feeling and behaving in a social situation.'

The education department of the University of Cambridge did not take much interest in the experiment at the time and one of their students, Mr A. J. Jenkinson, was later very critical that the students in the department were not told of the existence of the school, which he would very much like to have been allowed to visit.

Susan was not only deeply absorbed in interested observation of the sayings and doings of the children and in participating in their discoveries when such help would further their purposes but was also able to enjoy the society of those whom she called her 'child companions'. Children were not only an absorbing intellectual interest but also a genuine delight to her. Whenever she referred in her lectures to one or other of the children it was with such sympathy and insight that those who listened felt as if the child were actually present. She maintained her interest in them long after they left the school and many became her friends in later life. When writing of the children's happiness in the school, Evelyn Lawrence said that 'a further important reason for it was the pleasure in their achievements and the warmth of affection of which, in a school run by Susan Isaacs, any child could always feel sure.'

Susan remained only four years at the school, after which she became aware that Geoffrey Pyke was finding it very difficult to accept the role he had himself assigned to her as the equivalent of Prime Minister of the school and she therefore judged it best to withdraw from it. Another Head was found but the school did not contribute much after Susan left and ultimately had to be closed as Pyke met with a financial disaster. Susan herself, with characteristic loyalty, spoke very little about any difficulties. I myself only learnt of them after Susan's death from Mrs Pyke and Nathan Isaacs who were, of course, closely involved. When Pyke died, Susan gave a most generous appreciation of him in a broadcast programme to his memory.

She returned to London and spent much time in the work of writing up the Malting House material. Its contribution was immense: for a full appreciation, it would be necessary to read Susan's two books *Intellectual Growth in Young Children* and *Social Development of Young Children* and, moreover, to realize also that much of the material of her two most widely known smaller books *The Nursery Years* and *The Children We Teach* also stemmed from her work there. She had preserved material for a third book giving case histories of the development of individual children. She never found time to write this book though for many years she did not give up the idea. Mr van der Eyken is contemplating writing a book on the Malting House School and has access to this material and also to papers preserved by Geoffrey Pyke. A film was made of the school, but it has unfortunately proved impossible to trace this, though many attempts have been made to do so.

The publication of *Intellectual Growth* which preceded *Social Development* had an immediate impact on the educational world. I was a lecturer in a training college when it appeared and remember an excited colleague showing me the book and saying 'You *must* read this! It shows that young children can think in the way we do and the difference is due to lack of experience not to lack of ability to think.' She was an English specialist who gave me generous help in supervision in infant schools, and such people were very ready to regard the young child not merely with kindly tolerance but with increased respect once their perception had been sharpened by Susan's penetrating analysis and presentation of the evidence gained from the recorded sayings and doings of the children. The book gives a wealth of data on the ways in which young children learn, think, reason, and imagine and how far their quest for discovery can take them.

Social Development of Young Children which followed was more startling at the time to the many readers who had not previously realized the normality of young children's concern with bodily processes and physiological matters and their accompanying emotions. In fact Susan told me that she was even advised by a well-wisher not to publish this material for the sake of her own reputation! She could never have been persuaded to suppress evidence and was wholly concerned with the need for all children to be understood. At that time, however, she felt that it might be more appropriate to give younger students the facts without the deeper interpretation of them which she included in this book.

In these days, however, the book does not seem to have an upsetting effect, probably because knowledge of the emotional life of young children is more widely spread and has come to be accepted. The book also contributes a very comprehensive picture of the variety of ways in which young children develop relationships with each other, the causes for quarrels and aggression, and the growth of friendly feelings and co-operation. She points out that though the hostilities produce the greatest number of dramatic episodes in the lives of young children, a larger proportion of their time is spent in harmonious and friendly play. This knowledge is reassuring to nursery school teachers who often get an opposite impression because they are required by the situation to attend more often to the dramatic episodes.

The swiftness of pioneer nursery and infant school teachers to appreciate the relevance of this material to their own work was remarkable when one thinks of the very difficult conditions under which their own work was done. The fact that they did not dismiss Susan Isaacs' findings as applicable only to very intelligent children taught in small groups was, I think, partly due to their own growing convictions that educational 'apparatus', however carefully planned and traded, was not enough to meet the child's quest for knowledge and that 'habit training' did not really solve the emotional problems. Susan Isaacs' help came just at the right time for these devoted and enthusiastic teachers. She led them to realise the seriousness of the child's interest in solving problems and the reality of his thinking when engaged in spontaneous play, and also to appreciate the intensity of the young child's feelings and the reality of their emotional needs.

Susan Isaacs herself said that she owed her educational ideas mainly to Froebel and Dewey and this may well be true, but she had the art of interpretation and of bringing theory into line with present day practice so that teachers felt it was from her that they really understood the meaning of Froebel's words 'Play is not trivial but highly serious and of deep significance.' As one very gifted infant teacher put it, 'She interpreted Dewey better than he interpreted himself.' Susan began with the children and led teachers to observe, record, and understand their needs and to evolve their educational theory from this experience and

73

thought. She helped them to achieve the delicate and sensitive balance between when to stand aside in order to let the child make his own discoveries and when to support and help, so that he was not faced with failure and despair. She also showed them the very rich possibilities of following up the purposes of the children themselves in a good environment for learning. The kind of teacher who might have said 'If I don't start teaching reading, writing, and arithmetic to very young children what on earth *am* I to do with them?' could find many answers in Susan Isaacs' books.

I have heard many expressions of appreciation of her work from thoughtful and practical teachers and will quote a few in their own words.

'She demonstrated and interpreted child-centred education not only in a practical way, but also in a way which made the underlying psychology clear to me.'

'To me her greatest contribution is that she helped me to understand the nature and function of play and how to help others to understand it. Her book *Intellectual Growth in Young Children* is as valuable today as it ever was and answers the modern teacher's problems.'

'She gave teachers confidence to regard play as an absolute essential and redeemed it from any suggestion of triviality. She showed the dignity and place of play in a child's *total* development (emotional and physical, not only intellectual). She helped teachers to know how to look at children and their play and to use their observations to support and further the child's development. Her way of keeping records helped teachers to write them – to show how something originated and how the teachers participated, how to maintain the balance of when to come in and when to stand aside, how teachers need to work with the children but one step ahead. She showed teachers the "allness" of children and that what helps one side of a child helps other sides too. One can separate the values in order to talk about them but her work enabled teachers to see them working together.'

Though, at first, it was the outstandingly thoughtful teachers who were aware of Susan Isaacs' work, their influence spread to many others and gradually, in not few but many nursery and infant schools, periods for play which had before been permitted only at times when children needed rest from 'work' moved into a central place in the school programme and the time allowed for it was greatly increased. The nursery school teachers in particular, but many infant school teachers too, came to realize that children went further in discovery and learnt more by generous provision for play with the support of skilled teachers than they had done by being given instructions in groups or limited occupations with specially selected apparatus.

Susan Isaacs' work at the Malting House School may, therefore, be claimed as one of the great influences on the education of children under seven in the State schools of this country. That influence is now spreading upwards into the junior schools. It is probable that by now few teachers are aware of how much the influence originated from her work. The early pioneers were keenly aware of it and other teachers learnt from them and ascribed the credit to them, a matter about which Susan herself would have had no regret. Indeed she herself would have ascribed the credit to the pioneer teachers who had made it possible for children to learn this way in large classes, often under difficult conditions. What is, however, a matter for regret is that more teachers who are struggling with problems inherent in a way of educating children which requires clear thinking from the teacher have not read *Intellectual Growth in Young Children*, where they would find the answers to many of their questions.

5 · Fulfilment

(ii) The Department of Child Development

The six years from 1927 when Susan Isaacs left the Malting House School till 1933 when she was appointed Head of the newly formed Department of Child Development at the University of London Institute of Education were intensely active ones, largely occupied in a tremendous output of very significant writing and in undertaking a fresh training for psycho-analytic work. It was characteristic of Susan's thoroughness that when she became convinced of the value and importance of the work of Melanie Klein she decided, despite her senior status in the Society and the fact that she was already qualified to take patients for analysis, to begin at the beginning again and undertook a further analysis herself with Mrs Joan Riviere. She also took patients and was appointed by Professor Cyril Burt in a part-time capacity to supervise advanced psychology students at University College. She devoted a great deal of time to their supervision as well as to lecturing there and at Morley College for Adult Education and doing a considerable amount of other lecturing and editorial work. It is little short of miraculous that she found time during these years to publish her four most well-known books as well as a considerable number of articles, and also to make a weekly contribution to the journal *The Nursery World* where she answered the questions of parents and nurses with the greatest wisdom and insight. She began this service in 1929 and continued to give it after her appointment to the Department of Child Development until 1936. *The Nursery World* preferred authors to use a pseudonym and suggested the name 'Jane Strong'. Susan demurred at this as sounding much too authoritarian and dogmatic and Nathan to whom she confided her perplexity about what to be called produced the suggestion of 'Ursula Wise' which she immediately accepted. My sister who, as a trained children's nurse, was at that time a reader of *The Nursery World*, frequently said to me that I ought to read the letters by Ursula Wise as she was sure I would approve of them. I promised to do so, but being pre-occupied with other reading in connection with my appointment as a lecturer in education put the journals aside for later reading, and thereby lost my opportunity of becoming acquainted with Susan Isaacs earlier than I did. When I discovered who the author was I read them with avidity and felt the more regret that I had not done so before. Though in 1936 she ceased contributing to this journal, she never ceased to receive letters from parents about their children and was answering these personally right up to the time of her last illness. Many of them would fully justify publication and are as relevant to the needs of parents today as at the time when they were written. No service, in her view, ranked as more important than that of helping parents who were in need of advice about their children, and she brought all her knowledge and experience to bear: giving deep consideration to the nature of any problem and offering advice with discernment and sympathy in a way which helped parents to understand for themselves and therefore to feel more confident and less anxious, though she never minimized the difficulties either of the child or the parent. It was her respect for both, together with her vivid appreciation of the reality and intensity of a young child's feelings, which made her advice so acceptable and so fruitful to parents.

The Nursery Years which appeared in 1929 is regarded by many as her masterpiece and has been read by parents all over the world. It had been translated into many languages at the time of Susan's death and there have been several more translations since. It is also very much read by children's nurses and students in training for teaching and for work as housemothers in childrens' homes. It was awarded a medal by the Parents' Institute

77

in America as the best book for parents for the year (i.e. the American edition 1937). The book loses nothing in depth by being expressed in very simple and indeed most beautiful English. Susan herself felt happy about this book and though in later editions of her other work, she often wanted to make revisions and rejected a request for a revision of her *Introduction to Psychology*, on the grounds that it was now out of date, she never felt it necessary to revise or alter *The Nursery Years*.

In 1931 *Intellectual Growth in Young Children* appeared and in the following year *The Children We Teach* which is her only book specifically on the older child, from six years old upwards. It is also very widely read especially by teachers and students in colleges of education. In 1933 the second of her great Malting House contributions *Social Development of Young Children* followed. An examination of the bibliography will reveal the great number of articles and pamphlets which she had already published and which she continued to contribute but she was not able again to find time to write any more books until the last years of her life when physical illness removed her from most of her other responsibilities and she then wrote two more. Two of her great regrets were that she had not had the time to write the third book on the Malting House material or a book on adolescence which she much wished her life could be prolonged enough for her to do.

It would not have been surprising if these years of intense activity had left her no time for social pleasures, but this was not so. She even left herself time for sheer amusement. Nathan said, 'She loved being with friends, and had a great zest for charades and a most lively and infectious sense of fun which endeared her to everyone. For a great number of years she was an enthusiastic player of the game of demon or racing patience, revelling at its pace when at its most terrific, and usually leading and winning the race.' Her home was the meeting place for many friends who often gathered there for the pleasures of gracious hospitality and very satisfying intellectual discussion that ranged over many

78

subjects of current interest. On these occasions Susan was essentially more a listener than a talker though when she contributed it was always discerning and illuminating and showed her deep appreciation of every question which had been under discussion. She and Nathan, in smaller gatherings, would sometimes oppose each other forthrightly in argument while pausing occasionally to exchange an affectionate smile – their enormous respect for each other never made them feel committed to a need to accept each other's views on every subject and they sometimes did not do so, but such differences never interfered with their affection.

Joan Maurer told me that soon after she left her training college, Susan invited her to spend a week with her in London. She writes: 'I had never been to London before and the whole experience was quite a landmark in my life. Susan took me round on the tops of buses for a day with a map to help me to get my bearings, then sent me out to visit places of interest on my own and introduced me to interesting friends every evening. I don't think any grown-up had, before this, treated me naturally as the adult I felt I was. I was interested in the way Nathan and Susan were taking turns at earning enough to keep them, while the other partner did some research or writing; and in the smooth arrangements they had made to give them as much time as possible for their work. This did not exclude a rich social life, however, nor the relaxation they knew they needed.'

Susan made many friends through her various educational and psycho-analytic spheres of work and among these friendships was a long standing one with Sir Percy Nunn, then Director of the University of London Institute of Education. After she came to London again they discussed on several occasions the need to establish in England a centre for advanced study of Child Development and for research in the subject, such as existed in some other countries, and notably in America.

By the end of 1932 Sir Percy was convinced that the time was ripe for putting up a proposal to the Delegacy of the Institute of Education to ask for such a department to be established. He then asked Susan whether in the event of agreement from the University she would be willing to accept appointment as head of the new department. Her reply reveals how deeply her interests were by then involved in the work of psycho-analysis. Her realistic and vivid imagination led her to realize that such a department must inevitably grow and expand, so that the fact that in the first instance she was being asked only for part-time co-operation scarcely weighed with her and she most regretfully declined to accept the suggestion. On 28 December 1932 she wrote:

Dear Sir Percy,

Since your very kind talk with me three weeks ago I have been thinking very deeply and carefully about the personal situation which your splendid suggestion to me compels me to face. I want very much to make my position really clear to you, and am sure you will forgive my going rather deeply into personal motives.

First of all let me say that I appreciate your most gratifying invitation to me far more deeply and warmly than I can possibly say. With a very large part of myself I have a great wish to come and join you at the Institute of Education. The work you hold out to me would be in many ways *the* fulfilment of all my previous hopes and efforts. I love teaching, and I know I can do it. I should be extremely happy to work with you and for you, and I should feel it the greatest privilege to be allowed to do so.

The actual ripening of the ideas, which of course I have known for some time were a *possibility*, has, however, compelled me to face the fact that to undertake this work would definitely mean my relinquishing analytic work altogether, not necessarily at once, but certainly within a year or so. The work you envisage for me would very soon, if it were to be properly done, have to take up almost my full time, and eventually my whole time. Moreover, educational work and analytic work are not really

Susan aged 10

Officials of Women's Union – Manchester University, 1911. Susan on far right

compatible within one person's life, since the latter demands a special attitude and a very serious and continuous study of technique, even if one's time is not actually filled with patients. It involves quite a different mental attitude from teaching, lecturing and organizing, and cannot therefore be effectively carried out as part-time work. I do not of course mean that one cannot undertake courses of lectures on other aspects of psychology, whilst doing psycho-analysis. One certainly can do so, and I hope to continue doing so. I mean that one cannot do analysis as a part-time and subsidiary piece of research, while one's major activities are in educational directions.

I am thus faced with a definite decision between the two interests which have for many years filled my mind. I can no longer hope to hold them together, but must be willing to identify myself fully with the one or the other.

You will readily believe that this has been an extremely difficult choice for me. Since we met my mind has been occupied with nothing else, and I have had to review the situation in the light of everything that I know about my own personal wishes and deeper motives.

Since I first wrote to you three years ago to ask whether you might ever be able to consider such a possibility as you have now unfolded before me, I have gone a great deal further in my own experience of analytic technique. During the last nine months or so, I have had a taste not only of the satisfaction that comes from giving real help to minds in doubt and distress, but also gained a deep sense of the fundamental psychological research which the analytic technique with very young children makes possible, into the springs of thought and action. It is this further experience which has made me realize that that particular type of research is, above all things, the satisfaction I most seek. And after far more intense heart-searching than I can convey to you, I have had to come to the conclusion that I cannot bear to give up the work of analysis. You will realize the strength of this feeling when I tell you that my husband was very anxious that I should undertake the work with you, and that I have had to resist not only my own sense of the great importance of the opportunity you offer me, and of the deep pleasure it would give to me to work with you, but also his most eloquent and forcible statements of what that opportunity would mean. In spite of this, however, I cannot evade the fact that this intimate contact with individual minds, whether children or adults, and the opening for really fundamental psychological research which this gives me, weighs most heavily in the end. I feel sure you will understand that I should not be able to take such a choice without deep certainty that this was the right thing for me to do.

I am overwhelmed at the thought of saying 'no' to your suggestion, and any disappointment or inconvenience I may cause to you through this refusal. If I could have chopped myself in two and done both, I would have done that any time this last three weeks! And I have put off this choice and put it off, until I cannot in decency postpone it any longer. But when it actually came to the point, I had to choose the work of analysis.

I can only hope that in the end this will not prove anything more than a temporary inconvenience to you, and that you will soon find someone who will be able to carry on the great work which you open up, far more ably and surely than I could do. It will always, however, remain one of my permanent satisfactions to know that you were willing to give me such an opportunity. Will you forgive me?

With deepest regrets, and always my sincerest wishes for your own great work,

Yours very sincerely,

SUSAN ISAACS

Fortunately, however, for the future of the Department of Child Development, a week's further reflection after writing this letter brought second thoughts and Susan wrote again on 6 January 1933:

Dear Sir Percy,

May I return to the subject? I have been so deeply grieved at the idea of not working with you at the Institute that I have gone on thinking about the problem ever since I wrote to you. And a possibility has occurred to me that I had not envisaged before.

If my letter has not already led to your making other dispositions, either in action or in your own wishes, I should like to consider this possibility further.

Your suggestions opened up such vistas of development to me that, until this last day or two, I had approached the whole problem from the point of view of full-time work, at any rate in the future. But it has now occurred to me to consider more closely the fact that it *is* only part-time work for, probably, the next three or four years. And since I now do a good deal of various kinds of lecturing in addition to my analytic work with patients, I might perhaps, by withdrawing from these other commitments, be able to gather all these diverse efforts of time and energy together into one, and thus be able to give you fully what is needed. The idea had only to occur to me to appeal immensely – it seems, from *my* point of view, just the solution to my problem. I should be much happier to have my energies and interests unified in this way, and for such an end. The Institute is much the most appropriate place for me, and I should feel my work there to be so much more fruitful.

I have therefore been going over the practicability of withdrawing from these other commitments this summer, and believe, on consideration, that I could do so. It would mean asking Professor Burt to allow me to transfer myself from University College to the Institute. I have not said anything to him yet, but I do not doubt that he would forgive me, as he has the welfare of the Institute at heart too. (I suppose the lectures would in any case be inter-collegiate, so that his students could attend.) It would also mean finding someone to take over a Tutorial Class I began at Toynbee Hall this year, but I think I know someone who would do this as well as I can, and who would be glad of the chance, so that I could withdraw without doing any harm. And with the time gained from these and one or two other minor sources, it seems to me now that I could undertake the work for you, whilst it was a part-time responsibility.

In the three or four years before the Department of Child Development could afford a full-time head, we might well be able to find or train someone who would be the right person for the appointment. And you might perhaps even then care to retain me for separate courses of lectures.

If you would thus allow me to do whatever I can to build up the Department in this way, I should be only too delighted to take whatever steps are necessary to free my time. (I would not, of course, make more than tentative inquiries until your plans were official.)

It may, however, seem to you impracticable to begin the work on any other basis than the *intention* of full-time responsibility, should finances allow. I should quite understand this. It may indeed be so. But I felt I should like to raise this possibility with you, as soon as it occurred to me; and should be most happy if you felt the suggestion to be feasible.

Yours very sincerely,

SUSAN ISAACS

Sir Percy replied:

8th January 1933

Dear Mrs Isaacs,

At the time when the east wind raged in December, my constant foes, bronchitis and influenza, both saw their chance and laid me low. Immediately before Christmas I was judged well enough to leave London for convalescence and have been carrying out that process in the west of England. Your first letter reached me there some days ago and was a severe blow. I understood perfectly your point of view but, having from the beginning thought of the child-psychology department as *yours*, your decision that you could not be concerned with it naturally caused me lively disappointment. I ought to have acknowledged the letter at once; but to tell the truth I did not feel equal to any business, least of all business so painful, so postponed writing until my return home.

I have this evening arrived home, and am delighted to have your most kind letter giving your generous second thoughts upon the subject. I had decided, after the first letter, to go no farther with the project for the next year or two. Your second letter has, however, determined me to push on with it with all the vigour I had intended to bring to bear upon it. This means that I shall discuss it with Lord Eustace Percy, my chairman, bring it before my Delegacy at the next meeting, and urge the Delegacy to consider whether, even in the present unfavourable financial situation, a start cannot be made. It will be definitely helpful, not a hindrance, that if we can make a start at all you would be available only for part-time.

You will understand, of course, that everything must be regarded for the present as non-committal. What I tell you expresses my wishes and hopes, but the Delegacy has the last word. I greatly hope, however, that we may be able to start next session a department which would enjoy at least the very great advantage of your initiation, even if, when you have put it on its feet, it has to continue under other guidance.

I will seek an early opportunity of talking over the subject with Professor Burt as well as with others who may be interested. The lectures and seminars I have in view will be essentially inter-collegiate and I think that, as you say, Professor Burt will agree that they should be in the Institute. Before the beginning of the present session we had already reached an informal agreement upon the matter.

During the next few days I must continue to take things easily and shall not be in evidence at the Institute; but I shall pursue this most important question as soon and as diligently as I can. Meanwhile please receive my very warm acknowledgement of your kindness and consideration.

Yours sincerely,

T. PERCY NUNN

The Delegacy of the Institute of Education to which Sir Percy Nunn referred was a body on which the University of London was strongly represented. It included the Vice-Chancellor, the Chairman of Convocation, the Principal of the University, and five members of Senate, in addition to representatives of the Institute of Education of King's College, the London County Council, and other co-opted members.

Sir Percy Nunn was successful in obtaining consent to the proposed department. Indeed, at an earlier stage when the transference of the London Day Training College to the University was under discussion, the following paragraph appeared in the Statement of Policy and was adopted by the Senate:

'(e) Child Development: It is not desirable that the Institute at its training college level should add to its present activities by training teachers of young children. It should, however, have a department whose aim would be to enlarge and improve the scientific foundations upon which the education of young children should be based. Work in this direction of outstanding importance has been done in other quarters of the world but that is not a good argument for leaving it untouched in London. The results obtained by foreign observers almost always contain elements affected by the national *milieu*. It would, accordingly, be unsafe to apply them without qualification to the education of English children. In any case, the position enjoyed by young children here ought to make the contribution of English pedagogy to this subject one of more substantial importance than it has hitherto been. As in other departments of educational work, we can show some admirable practice, but the underlying principles have been insufficiently thought out and explored. Here is a valuable piece of work for the Institute to do. In particular, there are needed in the Training Colleges women of good academic and scientific training in pedagogy to take charge of the departments for training teachers of infants. The department of the Institute would attempt to supply that need, working in collaboration with other existing institutions concerned with the training of infants' teachers. It would be most desirable that it should have at its disposal a small school to be a place of observation and experiment such as those in Geneva, Yale University, Toronto and elsewhere, from which many valuable results have come. Such a school might possibly be attached to the other Institutions for Child Welfare which it is hoped to establish on the Foundling Hospital site.'

In March 1933 at a meeting of the Delegacy under the Chairmanship of Lord Eustace Percy, the scheme for establishing the Department in the following session was finally approved. During the negotiations which followed, Professor Burt played a leading part, not only by his generosity in agreeing to the transfer of Susan's work to the Institute of Education, but by working to overcome what he described as 'old fashioned prejudices' on the part of some members of the Delegacy to the idea of her appointment. Susan herself ascribed the fact that in England there was no severe separation between the findings of psycho-analysis and the work of teachers to the influence of people like Sir Percy Nunn and Sir Cyril Burt who were able to appreciate the contribution of psycho-analysis to all those who needed to understand the emotional as well as the intellectual needs of children. They did not share the view which was at that time commonly held in certain parts of Europe, that the teacher's function was solely to impart knowledge, while concern with a child's emotions and mental health must be left entirely to clinical workers dealing with disturbed children.

In May 1933 Sir Percy was in correspondence with the Board of Education whose cordial support was forthcoming. In one letter he writes of Susan Isaacs: 'You will see that she made an excellent beginning by taking a brilliant degree under Samuel Alexander. What I have always admired in her is a combination of practical good sense and experience with philosophic thoroughness.'

He refers to the two chief objectives of the new Department as (i) to supply the demands of the more progressive training colleges with experienced people 'equipped scientifically' to become lecturers in infant school education and (ii) to create a centre for research in the field of child development and infant pedagogy.

It is clear that financial stringency interfered with some of the original plans. Before a final decision was taken he had written in a letter to the Principal of the University, Dr E. Dellar, of his hopes that the Laura Spelman Rockefeller Foundation might be disposed to help since this body had expressed interest at an earlier stage.

He also wrote: 'It would be essential to secure an able and highly qualified woman to co-ordinate and conduct the work as a whole, to give some of the most important teaching and to carry out and inspire research. There is such a woman in Mrs Susan Isaacs, M.A., D.Sc., who has just received a part-time appointment in Professor Burt's Department. I have explored this question very thoroughly and I find that all the competent people I have consulted not only agree, but agree most cordially with my own opinion that Mrs Isaacs has outstanding qualifications for the position I am describing. Her writings alone show that she can hold her own with the best authorities in the theory and practice of her subject either here, on on the continent, or in the United States. If we could give her favourable opportunity within the Institute her activities could hardly fail to redound greatly to its credit. The most suitable arrangement would probably be to give her a half-time appointment in the Institute carrying with it the title either of Professor or of Reader. She is good enough for a professorship but it might be possible to afford only a readership. In brief, the alternatives seem to me to be a half-time professorship at £500, or a half-time readership at say £300.

'As regards assistant staff it would probably be enough to start with a research assistant who would "devil" for Mrs Isaacs and I should think that a salary of £250 to £300 would be adequate. If the department grew it would be necessary to add another teacher but I think that at the beginning the only special

88

teaching we would need to provide would be that of the head of the department, the other teaching would naturally be supplied by the general staff of the Institute.

'(b) In connexion with research the important provision needed is a school for the observation of infants and study of methods of handling them in their tender years. I have in view the kind of provision which Professor Gesell has, or Professor Bott at Toronto, or Professor Piaget at Geneva. Essentially it means that we want help to establish a voluntary nursery school with space and the proper technical arrangements for observing the ways of little children and their behaviour under standard conditions and the conditions favourable to their intellectual as well as their physical development.'

In Susan Isaacs' day many of the proposals in Sir Percy's mind did not materialize. She did not even obtain a readership and her salary was never more than £325 with an allowance of £100 for a secretary. Despite a large number of appeals to various trusts she never obtained what she so much hoped for – a grant to establish a 'laboratory' in the form of a nursery school and though in her last few years in the department she made out a strong and convincing case for an assistant lecturer it was not successful and she was therefore obliged to refuse good applicants for the course and keep the numbers small. Her magnificent work was carried out with a minimum of facilities. It was only in her last year that she even had a telephone in her room, and she had to go down and up a great many stairs if anyone rang her up. It was well for the department's interests that she was a person who had made a fine art of surmounting difficulties and also was so well liked and respected that she was able to attract much voluntary co-operation and the services of distinguished people who accepted very small fees for the interest and pleasure of working with her. The amount of sheer physical effort involved was, however, very great. She paid personal visits to many schools and clinics in order to obtain help for her students. She was appointed in May 1933 and at once engaged in the task of building up the courses, securing lecturers, and interviewing applicants for the session which began in the October of that year. I was one of the earliest applicants and had been granted an interview with Sir Percy Nunn, during the course of which he telephoned to Susan and she came to join us. It was the first time I met her and I was at once aware of her charm and courtesy. She discussed the possibilities of my being able to take the main lectures and seminars since I could not be released more than part-time from my work at Bishop Otter College in Chichester where I was a lecturer in Education. I was the only intending student who wished to complete the full course, spreading it over two years by obtaining part-time release and she suggested that as it would also suit people who wanted to take one or others of her main lectures and seminars only as 'occasional' students, she would place these as far as possible on Friday evenings and Saturday mornings. As I should be able to obtain release from mid-day on Friday till mid-day on Monday this suited me extremely well. She also told me what would be available at the other times when I should be free. I remember asking, in a rather dazed fashion, whether I was accepted for the course and she said 'Yes', and I found myself outside walking as if in a dream! I had long wished for such an opportunity to go much deeper in the study of child psychology than I had ever had the chance to do and I was, at that stage, still a non-graduate, though I had taken the Froebel diploma for the training of teachers. In later days I mentioned my astonished delight at having been so easily 'accepted' for the course and Susan expressed amusement to which I replied 'You have no idea what it meant to a non-graduate to be accepted by a University.' She refrained from pointing out that in fact she had a very good idea of it indeed! In the first term there were only five full-time students, one, like myself, a lecturer in a training college. Two others, I think, joined later in the year as full-time students. They were all interesting people who through very varied experience had arrived, like myself, at a stage when the need to know more about children had become an insistent desire, and who had been waiting for such an opportunity. There was a larger group of very able people who attended single courses or one or two seminars taken by Susan Isaacs herself. Two of these were inspectors of the Board of Education.

Susan's attitude was one of great flexibility over allowing people to use the course for their own individual needs and purposes. Anyone taking the full course would have been required to lead seminars and also, if they wanted to obtain the certificate, to undertake an individual study or research, but she was equally interested in those who were not concerned with obtaining a certificate. Later, when applications became too numerous, it was necessary to refuse some suitable applicants for the full-time course, but I do not think she ever refused any suitable applicant for attendance at lecture courses. The main course of lectures in Child Development were always given to fairly large audiences which included students from University College. Occasionally people applied to take the course or to attend lectures when they were not sufficiently qualified to benefit from an advanced course, and though she firmly maintained standards and so did not admit them, she often went to considerable trouble to help them find teaching more suitable for their needs.

During the six years when the course was under her direction British students seldom received financial help. Some people from other countries were aided by their education authorities. The prospect of release of English teachers on salary did not appear for very many years even after her retirement. In fact, my own opportunity to ask for part-time release was made possible by my knowledge that the college was in financial difficulties caused by two cuts in the number of teachers who could be accepted for training which followed close upon a direction to colleges to enlarge their accommodation, so I knew that any means of economizing on my salary would be welcome at that stage. Owing, however, to the generosity of my Principal, Miss E. T. Bazeley, the reduction was a small one and I was definitely one of the lucky ones who did not have to solve such problems as whether to forego lunch in order to afford the fare to visit a distant school! Susan, well aware of our difficulties, did everything possible to minimize our expenses and the Institute's fees were modest. The lack of help and the fact that the course carried no official qualification did at least ensure that the people who chose to take it were motivated solely by the wish to learn. Enthusiasm was high, not the less so perhaps because people had saved their money strenuously in order to afford to be free to study. A disadvantage, however, was that men could very seldom afford it and most of the men students were overseas people on grant from their own countries. For this reason the strong influence which Susan Isaacs' work had in humanizing the teaching of psychology in the training colleges took much longer to reach the men's colleges in this country. A great many of the early students took up lectureships in colleges soon after completing the course and others were already engaged in this work when they entered the department.

In the first year Susan arranged regular tutorial sessions with all full-time students, but after that, numbers rose and she was unable to do this any longer in the time available in her part-time appointment. She would, however, always see students individually on request and she arranged a tea-gathering in her room every week for all those who wanted to come and talk to her then.

The main fields of study included:

(1) A three term course of lectures on the psychology of infancy and early childhood (till about nine years of age).
(2) Seminars on:
    (a) The educational bearings of the facts of child development.
    (b) Problems and methods of research in child development.
    (c) The teaching of child psychology to students in training colleges.
    (d) Mental hygiene of children.
    (e) Mental testing.

These were all conducted by Susan Isaacs herself. There was also a short course on the physiology of growth conducted in the first year by Professor Harris and subsequently by Professor Samson Wright, and another on the medical care of children which, after the first year, was continued for many years by Dr Flora Shepherd. Professor Hamley conducted a seminar on the interpretation of statistics. In the first year Susan conducted this herself.

Students also attended Professor Percy Nunn's lectures on Principles of Education and Professor Hamley's on Educational Psychology. In the second year Dr Winnicott gave two special lectures, for students in the department only, on the psychological factors in the physical welfare of young children, and later both the number of lectures and scope of his subject were considerably expanded.

Practical work included:

(1) Systematic observation of children in nursery schools followed up by weekly discussion periods with Susan Isaacs.
(2) Observation and some participation in a child guidance clinic.
(3) For students who were qualified and who chose to do so, the undertaking of some actual research under direction. Some students, however, preferred to make special studies of more general topics.

In 1948, when Susan died, I was asked by the *New Era* to contribute to their obituary article by writing of her work in the department, and this caused me to revive my memories of my own period in the department, not then so far behind me, as I had continued my association with it for three years, that is till 1936. I wrote: 'My own experience of her teaching was gained when I became her student in this first year of the department's existence. We were a privileged group, because there were so few of us, and from such varied fields of experience, that we could not fail to get to know her very well

93

and to admire the skill with which she met our individual needs.

'My most vivid recollections are of the many ways in which she led us to do our own thinking; of superb teaching, but also of wise silences until we had worked out a problem to a point where her help became essential and we could really assimilate it. A seminar to which students had come without adequate preparation could be an embarrassing situation and seldom occurred more than once in any one year! She had no intention of doing our thinking for us, but when we had done our proper part of the work, with what crystal clarity was her help most fully and generously given. She gave us so much, not only by her vivid speech, with its unerring choice of the perfect word to express full meaning, and by the artistry of her lecturing, but by the questions which set our minds working, by requests to "be more specific" when our statements became vague or ambiguous, and by a certain twinkle in the eye when we gave evidence of prejudiced thinking or wilful disregard of evidence. She made us laugh at ourselves and face issues with honesty. She was patience and courtesy incarnate with the naïve but honest question, but could show firmness and even on rare occasions a touch of severity with mere pretentiousness. She had the rare art which could combine supreme ability to draw out the shy and sensitive student with a power which quelled without hurting the loquacious and caused him (or her!) to produce the one grain of thought hidden in a bushel of words.

'She took great pleasure in the presence every year of students from other countries and welcomed the contribution they made to the knowledge of the English people. She was quick and generous in her appreciation of what was valuable in current research in other countries and immediately made it known to her students. Moreover, she encouraged people in this country who were doing valuable work to publish it, and for this purpose edited the series "Contributions to Modern Education" for Methuen, the standard of which she kept consistently high. She also had a most generous and warm appreciation of what was sound or original in her students' own work, and her genuine personal enjoyment of useful material and knowledge which we contributed from our various fields of experience was something to warm the heart. She gave us, too, the pleasure of knowing that she enjoyed our company and the social occasions when she invited us to her home were gay events never to be forgotten. Yet there was no one more comforting in times of personal sorrow or more ready to give full support or wise counsel in matters of professional difficulty.

'Her dignity was so much part of herself that she never needed to protect it by formal conventionalities. During my second year, when I could be in London only at week-ends, most of my tutorials with her took place in an "A.B.C." over cups of coffee, and the amount of invaluable help that I received in this unconventional setting left me awed by her ability to use to capacity the odd half-hour – her only interval in a busy day before a big public lecture. In those early days, when the Institute was in Southampton Row, the department had only scanty accommodation, and I well remember her amusement when an enthusiastic American visitor called to look at her "set up" and she had little to show him except the chairs and tables. When the Institute moved into the new quarters in the University of London she took great delight in its increased facilities. She undertook all the additional work necessary in order to organize, staff and equip a playroom in the Institute where small children could meet daily and play under skilled supervision, thus giving the students opportunities to watch and get to know them. She once said to me how much easier it would have been for the University to understand if she had happened to want mummified babies from Ancient Egypt!

'As the inheritor of her files I came to realize very clearly what an immense amount of work she covered during those six years when she held her post at the Institute in a "part-time" capacity. Her enormous correspondence with many countries and in answer to countless inquiries which ranged from the highly technical questions which required memoranda in reply, to the very individual and personal requests for help about people's careers and their children's problems, was answered with scrupulous care and courtesy. She also somehow found time to meet the many new public responsibilities which came to her through her position in the department, as well as those which inevitably followed her in her personal capacity. While sorting the many papers which belong to the three years when I was myself a student, I marvelled again at the way in which she never gave us the sense that she was hurried or too busy to attend to the needs of her students and her many visitors from all over the world.

'One of her greatest wishes and hopes was that the department should become a centre of serious research, and she did all in her power to help any student who wished to continue investigations for which one year in the department was too short a time to do more than make a beginning. She rejoiced greatly in the award of the Leon research fellowship to one of her ex-students and in the recent awards of two research fellowships, one from the Elmgrant Trust to the Chelsea Nursery School and the other from the Nuffield Foundation to the Nursery School Association, both of which are being conducted in close co-operation with the Department of Child Development.

'She spent much time and energy in trying to win further facilities which would help investigations into the psychology and education of young children, and although some of her efforts did not meet with immediate success she was convinced that a fuller recognition of the need for such work in this country would inevitably come one day. It gave her much happiness that she was able to see its beginnings.

'Students who, like myself, after completing the course in her department, were privileged to work as research students under her direction, found it an inspiring experience, for not only was her swift appreciation of scientific issues so masterly and so clarifying, but her creativeness and sense of adventure in exploring new ground gave us courage to surmount many difficulties. It was appropriate that her degrees were in both

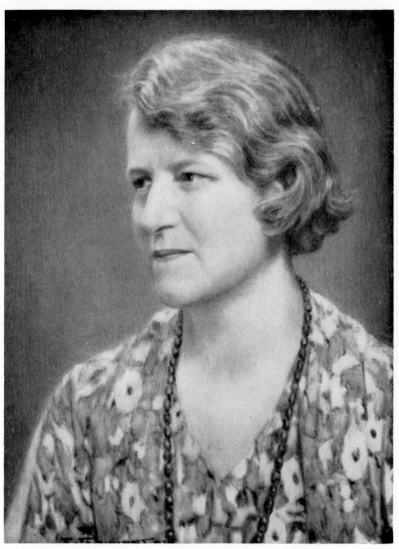

Susan in 1935
Photographed from a miniature painted
by her brother, Enoch Fairhurst

science and arts, because one could not work with her without acquiring the discipline of the scientist nor listen to her without a keen sense of being in the presence of an artist. Her attitude was fully scientific and her love of children free from any trace of sentimentality, but to hear her speak of a child and to quote his sayings was as if the living child, with his perplexities and difficulties, his loving and hostile feelings, and through all, his freshness and charm, were actually before us.'

As a tutor, Susan was superb. She identified herself completely with the students' need to find out and understand for themselves and encouraged their gropings for knowledge and insight with genuine respect for every discovery they made. My own experience was typical and illustrates well the kind of help she gave to her students' individual problems. At that stage, though my main wish was to study the techniques of research method and I should have been willing to do this on any subject of Susan's choice, she encouraged me to choose a topic which appealed to me, and the chief problem in my mind at the time was to try to find out how in the world play was able to help a 'difficult' child to become less difficult! I had discovered (at this stage of my ignorance, to my astonishment) that this strange phenomenon seemed to occur! I had taken some so-called difficult children into the play centre which I ran in Chichester with my students as helpers, but our motives were solely to give a good time to some of the children who lived in crowded homes and were our nearest neighbours, and I too had a second motive in that I felt it was a good way to help my students to get to know children more intimately than they could hope to do on teaching practice alone. I never imagined that we should be exercising 'good influence' until people began to tell us that certain difficult children were so much better since they came to us and we ourselves too became aware that problems were diminishing. I, however, had no idea why this should be so or how it occurred.

Whether Susan was surprised to find that even a Froebel trained teacher was still unaware of the therapeutic value of play or whether she had any temptation to hand over to me answers to my problems which were well known no doubt by clinical psychologists, I do not know, but she certainly revealed no such feelings if she had them. She was a perfect support to my own quest for finding out and would listen patiently when I gave her material from the play of children in the playrooms of child guidance clinics and tried, often in vain, to find a link between this play and the problems which I had learnt to be those of the children concerned. Only when I asked her specifically to do so would she interpret some of the behaviour and she later encouraged me to transfer my studies to my own play centre children about whom I knew much more, and work over their material with her. I was left with the feeling that any discoveries I made were really my own, though she was by no means detached – in fact I knew she was deeply interested and involved. It was, I felt, a partnership in inquiry and she generously ascribed all my discoveries to me and even persuaded me to write a book on the play centre. She was most generous in the way she would always acknowledge any help or interest which a student's work had been to her. I remember her keeping me back one day after a seminar I had led and saying, 'You do realize, don't you, how very valuable that was? It is what I have been so much wishing to hear put to people who train teachers.' After which, of course, I walked on air! No student who gave her their own thoughts and ideas ever had occasion to regret it. I was able recently to talk to Dr Lois Munro, a psycho-analyst, who had in her earlier days had experience of Susan as a supervisor when Dr Munro was undergoing her training as an analyst. I was deeply interested to find how similar her picture was to my own of Susan as a teacher. She said, 'Susan was devoted to helping *me* understand the material – one's comments to her left out her own viewing of the material. She fostered the learning and experience of her students and only put in her own views if asked. One felt very much "contained" by her because she would encourage one's exploration. She was a container of one's questing, but one was aware of her personality and that she wouldn't let herself be exploited and so one felt safe to ask her help. If she were not well she would say so. She did not pretend to greater strength than she had and herein lay her strength.'

Dr Munro referred to Susan's deep interest in her students' personality and mentioned how Susan had once told her that she was 'like a dog on the scent of a hare' but this, said Susan, was not a criticism and she appreciated it. Dr Munro also expressed very vividly what was so evident in all Susan's teaching, 'She had such a clear mind. She had the capacity to assimilate, correlate and order the material to make it clear for others to follow.' This was an ability that Susan had displayed from much earlier days. It was fully evident in her teaching of adults in tutorial classes. Where perhaps there was a difference in the way she taught at this later period was that in the early days students would say her criticism could be almost devastating, which was something I never knew of her work with students later. She was forthright and very clear in disposing of any unsound so-called 'evidence' and she led her students to be fully aware of the need for scientific safeguards and to avoid vague statements – but when I knew her this was done with such courtesy and sensitivity to our feelings that we never felt 'devastated'. I should doubt whether mature students are any less sensitive than younger ones so it seems that Susan herself may have mellowed in the way in which she expressed criticism.

The many letters written by Susan over her years in the department reveal the endless trouble she went to for every student. She arranged for their individual needs to be met by special visits, practical experience, and interviews with those who could help them most. She often supported them in finding suitable posts, sometimes long after they had completed the course, and gave further advice and help to them after they left. Her interest in them never ceased when they were no longer students and to the end of her life she rejoiced in hearing of their success. Many of them later became her close friends. I myself had that great privilege and was able also at a later stage to undertake further research with her assistance.

Susan's work in the department was by no means limited

entirely to work with and for her students. The wider world was quick to recognize the existence of a Department of Child Development. General advisory work poured in upon her. She was always interested that in the very first year of the department's existence she was asked to submit evidence required in relation to a trial for murder. A two-year-old child had fallen out of a railway carriage and the defence was that the child had played with and opened the door while the father was in the corridor; while the prosecution's case was that a child of that age would not have been capable of opening a door and, therefore, the father must have pushed her out. With characteristic thoroughness and with the co-operation of a nursery school, Susan was able to produce evidence that some railway carriage doors can be opened by some two-year-old children and the father was acquitted. Susan not only felt human sympathy for tragedy of the father's position and believed the acquittal to be right, but was also interested that the department should have won such speedy public recognition. The number of individuals and public bodies who sought her advice are too numerous to attempt to report. When one thinks how busy she quickly became some of them seem almost impertinent but Susan was never impatient and was aware that it was difficult for people to find help. She did not waste words but would always reply and some of her replies are masterpieces of brevity and adequacy. One head teacher of an infant school wrote (with a minimum of apology):

Dear Dr Isaacs,

I want a psychological definition of play. Would you give me one? I am giving a lecture on 'The Play Way with Infants' and find my own definition of play too limited.

Thanking you in anticipation of help.

Believe me,
Yours sincerely,
. . .

Susan replied:

Dear Miss X,

I would suggest that play is any activity of a child which is freely chosen and entered into spontaneously for its own sake, without reference to any end beyond itself. It makes no difference what the material of play is, it is the attitude of mind that defines it.

With all kind regards,

Yours sincerely,

. . .

Another, and characteristically careful, reply was written in answer to a much more courteously worded request from an Inspector of the Board of Education for advice on the use of fairy tales for young children.

Dear Miss X,

I always feel that the question of fairy tales for the modern child is a difficult one, and I don't believe there is any categorical answer to be given. It all depends! That is to say, I believe it to be a matter of age and individuality. I fully agree with you that the classical fairy tales are part of the literary heritage which children have a right to, and there is no doubt that for a great many children the standard fairy tales are valuable psychologically in precisely the same way in which great drama is for us. That is to say, they externalize the child's phantasies in a form that robs them of their individual terror. It is a help to the child to share these phantasies with other children and with grown-ups. The literary expression has the same function as the child's own dramatic play, and eases internal tension and enables the child to distinguish between phantasy and external reality. But there is no doubt that the more bloodthirsty ones, such as Red Riding Hood and Jack and the Beanstalk, can for (a) children below a certain age and (b) children of a certain psychological type, act as a piece of external reality, and thus reinforce phantasies and result in overwhelming terror. With regard to age, it does not seem to me possible to state the precise age common to all children; but it is the age at which the child has already come to a pretty clear distinction between 'pretend' and real. We know that the two-year-old has hardly got this distinction at all. Many three-year-olds have not got it, a larger number of four-year-olds have, and the majority of five-year-olds certainly have. I think I would not want to tell any of the more frightening fairy tales to any child under five, and I would never tell such a tale just before bed-time. It is, however, fairly safe to tell such tales to children of five and over individually, provided one can watch the reaction of the child and modify the story or cease to go any further with such stories if the child shows that he cannot bear it. When it comes to a group of children, however, it is far more difficult. One cannot be sure that in a class in school there will not be one or more children who are so neurotic that they cannot bear these stories. I would, therefore, want to put the age for telling such stories at least a year later, say six years of age. In the general way I think it would be safe to tell these stories to six-year-olds in an elementary school, since it is also true that the children would get a certain amount of relief and support from meeting the stories in common with other children, and I would always give the children the chance to play out such stories in dramatic action. I would consider this vitally important. In dramatic play it would be possible to pick out the children who were too sensitive and to give them some special reassurance by a humorous reference to the 'pretend' element in the story, or even in extreme cases of letting them join another group when such stories were to be told or played.

I don't believe that one does add new fears and excitements through telling such stories. They are already there, but as I have suggested the risk is in presenting them in so vivid a form or at such an early age that the child is unable to realize that they are only psychic material and do not represent real events.

Another aspect of the same problem that you do not touch upon is the question of films such as 'The Three Little Pigs'. I should be very cautious about taking tiny children to such films, since they strengthen the already overwhelming visual element in the phantasies. The Big Bad Wolf seems to me a terribly frightening figure. For a child over five it is of course a different matter.

I fully agree then that your general suggestion that the type of story of the 'Here and Now' story book should be the main pabulum for children of four and five years, but that plenty of the repetitive and milder type of fairy tales like 'The Old Woman with the Pig' may be used; and then for five and six-year-olds the more gruesome ones as an occasional, but to be thoroughly enjoyed, addition to literary experiences.

With all kind regards,

Yours sincerely,

. . .

Many of her letters were long and all were very careful and considered. They very rarely expressed impatience though she was firm in directing people to other sources of information if they expected too much; she would never allow her name to be used without being sure that the matter had her full approval and, as Dr Munro said, she did not allow herself to be exploited. There are very few letters which could be described as severe but there is one which conveys a stern reproof to a lady who offered her a commission for recommending a school which she had never seen! She was, however, prepared to go to the trouble of visiting a school if she had grounds for thinking it might prove to be a help to parents who asked her advice, but would never have accepted payment for such a service. She had, of course, to refuse many of the enormous number of requests for lectures which she received, but nearly always with genuine regret and she accepted more than most people would have thought possible. Her values emerge very clearly in what she would accept and priority was always given to the question of what was likely to offer the most significant help to children. She was also often willing to return hospitality to those who had received her students, sometimes by speaking at quite small and unofficial meetings of parents and teachers. In this and other connections too she maintained a close link with 'progressive' schools both inside and outside the state educational system. Their teachers were quick to recognize her as a champion of their cause and turned to her if in any difficulty or perplexity, being willing also to give a warm welcome to her and her students.

These teachers were also not only willing but eager to help her in any inquiry she might have in hand. It was through such co-operation that her wish to have a 'Laboratory Nursery School' eventually came near to being granted. Mrs Natalie Davis, an American mother, when she came to make her home in England, had wished to send her children to a nursery school but found there were none available at that time in the neighbourhood of Chelsea where she lived. She gathered together a small group of like-minded parents and they subscribed to buy two artists' studios and the adjoining historic cottage known in the district as 'King Henry VIII's Hunting Lodge', though the actual building is of the early Stuart period. The Chelsea Open Air Nursery School had been founded in 1927 and Mrs Davis was always eager to have it used for research. Very soon after Susan's appointment to the Department of Child Development, Mrs Davis wrote to ask her if she would care to use it and to send her students there. From the first year Susan always did this and the relationship with the school grew. Mrs Davis persuaded her to undertake its educational supervision, and the superintendent of the school was able to make reports to her and hold regular conferences with her. Finally Mrs Davis offered to hand over the entire educational direction of the school and the responsibility of appointing its staff to Susan who was then appointed as one of the trustees of the school. Soon after that, however, war broke out and the children were scattered, so the school was closed till 1944 and Susan herself had no further use of it, though she continued to help it and remained a trustee.

That so much of Susan's tremendous effort resulted in winning privileges not for herself as much as for her successor was a matter for which I feel a regret which she did not ever appear to share, though she had spent so much time and effort in fruitless appeals to trusts in the hope of having a department with greater facilities for research. There was no money available to staff the Chelsea School as the Malting House School had been staffed in order to have full records kept and data systematically collected, but the school has, nevertheless, been very valuable to the department. Susan never wasted energy on lamenting what could not be done but spent it on using to the full the opportunities which were available. I have already mentioned that in the last year of her period as head of the department when the space in the new university building gave her a room, she immediately started a small play group on the premises. Five out of her six years in the department were, however, spent in the old building in Southampton Row, where her sole accommodation was one room which she used both as her office and for students to study in when she was not occupying it herself. She put her own books and material at their disposal in this room.

To do justice to her very far-reaching activities in these years would be impossible in so short a book. A few, however, should not be omitted. She was asked to supply evidence for the 1934 Board of Education's Report on Nursery and Infant Schools and she wrote the chapter on the psychological development of children up to seven years, though she was disappointed that, in its final form, her material was cut up and sub-divided more than she would have approved. The Wiltshire Education Committee asked her help in evolving record cards for teachers to keep and these, together with their accompanying notes for teachers and the book *The Educational Guidance of the School Child* which expands this material, are still felt by some infant teachers to be more valuable than anything which has been suggested since. She also wrote for the Institute of Education's *Year Book in Education* her long article 'Psychological Aspects of Child Development' which is now available as a separate booklet (Evans Bros.). In 1936 she transferred her help in answering parents' questions to the journal *Home and School* because its editor, G. A. Lyward, for whom she had great regard and respect, led her to feel that in this way she might be able to help teachers as well as parents. She also gave help to Mrs Len Chaloner who was editing the journal *Parents*. As an editor she already had much experience and she now put this ability to the service of education, particularly in founding and editing the series published by Methuen which I have mentioned earlier, but she gave editorial help to many others, including people in the world of education, both here and in the U.S.A., while of course withdrawing nothing of such services from the fields of psychology and psycho-analysis.

In co-operation with the Home and School Council, she edited a series of pamphlets entitled 'Concerning Children' designed to help parents with the care and upbringing of infants but also dealing with normal problems and characteristic behaviour of older children, including adolescents, and sometimes with educational matters. She found authors, when necessary, for topics she judged to be most vital and wrote one of the pamphlets herself on 'The First Two Years'. This series brought a fierce attack on her – one of many from the same person – who wrote telling Sir Percy Nunn that the University was letting down its standards in giving the name of its Institute of Education to so trivial a series of publications. It was inevitable that, holding such a position with so much ease and unquestioned authority, Susan should incur some animosity which no doubt sprang from envy. One attempt was even made to usurp her position. Though she was too human not to feel indignant at unjustifiable attacks she was remarkably able to tolerate the situation and even showed generosity in her attitude, which was that provided she could firmly defend herself and what she stood for, she would be as helpful and as little hurtful as possible to those who attacked her. To one lady who was constantly writing hostile letters, she used the phrase: 'I am sorry it should trouble you that we have to agree to differ on this matter.' Though she never liked wounding anyone who was vulnerable, she could enjoy a battle in what she felt was a good cause and when I once told her this, she said, 'How did you find that out?' Whereat I produced a copy of a letter she had written to the *Spectator* in answer to a critic of a carefully considered review she had written of one of Adler's books. She wrote:

Sir,

I should like to assure Mr M. that I did not write my review of Adler's book in any ignorance of his other work nor the place which he holds in the minds of his followers. I have been familiar with his writings for many years, and with the history of his relation to Freud and the psycho-analytic movement. I have heard him lecture more than once; and as I wrote my review I had beside me one of his own most recent statements of the development of his psychology – his article on 'Individual Psychology' in *Psychologies of 1930*. My criticisms were considered and deliberate. And I follow Mr M. in asking readers to look again at the passages I quoted from the book. They speak for themselves, most eloquently, and I should not have quoted them had there not been many more like them.

'Constructive intentions' cannot be accepted as a justification of an inadequate psychology that makes such enormous claims for itself. We should not excuse the man who built a rotten bridge, just because he *wanted* to help people get across the river, especially if he claimed to be the maker of the latest and best bridges in the world! Of course Adler has the wish 'to relieve children of feelings of insufficiency and curtailment', but so have all serious educational psychologists. The valuable elements in Adler's psychology are in fact common to all who are interesting themselves in the child's point of view. It is this goodwill towards the child that wins people's attention; but Adler's special formulae have gained sympathy chiefly where the solid work of genuine investigators, more concerned with their science than with publicity, is not yet known.

I am sorry to have shocked Mr M. by using the adjective 'cruel'; but no amount of surface goodwill can justify the deliberate probing of the difficulties of a neurotic child in front of a large audience. However, it is perhaps even more silly than cruel. Only the most naïve psychologist would imagine that in such a situation he could possibly get below the surface of a child's mind.

And to try to use intelligence tests as a *means* of education, when the world is full of other things more suitable, could only be suggested by one who does not understand what they are. They are of course a delicate instrument, forged by vast labour and research, for the single purpose of measurement and diagnosis. To use them in the way Adler suggests is *not* constructive, for it throws away one of our sources of knowledge of the nature of the child's problem. Only when we have *understood* his difficulties can we begin to help him. But if we obscure the very instruments of understanding, how shall we know how to come to his aid?

She wrote a considerable number of reviews, many of which make most delightful reading, and though she always paid tribute to what was of value she certainly did not mince matters if she felt attack to be deserved. A few extracts from a review she wrote of a book on *Child Psychology*, first written in 1928 but revised in 1946, bring Susan Isaacs as I knew her very vividly to my mind.

This third edition takes account of many researches since that date. It provides a useful summary and discussion of recent work on such topics as the innate equipment of the infant, reflexes and random activities, habit, perceptual learning and memory. It is, however, a very uneven book. . . . The general bias is 'behaviouristic' in the narrow Watsonian sense. There is so little understanding of psychical functions as such that it is doubtful whether the book is rightly entitled *Child Psychology*.

To the reviewer, its main interest lies in its methodology. The author not only tends to think of complex mental processes mainly in 'behaviouristic' terms but jumps about from physiological to psychological modes of expression and back again, without apparently realizing that she is doing so.

If the poet asks:

> 'Tell me where is fancy bred
> Or in the heart or in the head?
> How begot how nourished?
> Reply reply'

Dr A. answers: 'Love' (as distinct from lust) 'is a series of co-ordinated reflexes controlled largely by the cranial division of the autonomic nervous system plus the perception of these changes together with the ideational content and the stimulus in response to which both appeared.' Is anyone really the wiser for this hybrid definition?

Not only are the emotions treated as essentially non-psychical: they are also enormously over-simplified. 'When the individual is in love, if it be love and not excitement, he is in an excellent physiological state. Digestion is at its best, the salivary flow is normal, the peristaltic contractions are balanced neither too rapid nor too slow.' This is contrasted with the effect of the 'sex drive', the two being kept quite apart until adolescence.

But Freud's work (to which, curiously enough, the author pays a limited tribute in her first chapter and at other points) has shown that 'love' and the 'sex drive' cannot be considered in this sharp separation and contrast. And in any case love is a highly complex state of mind – as the poets have always known. Whether or not it is directed to a consciously sexual object it commonly carries with it, as well as tenderness, joy and satisfaction, some measure of self-doubt, anxiety, insufficiency, incipient grief and dread of loss: 'infinite passion and the pain of finite hearts that yearn'.

The inadequacy of the author's account of human emotions is not made up for by the fragmentary 'behaviouristic physiology in terms of which she attempts to deal with human experience. Moreover, when questions arise which tend to stir affective responses in all who investigate them, objectivity goes to the winds, Dr A. swings naïvely between dogmatic denials of certain facts and practical warnings to parents as to how to prevent these denied phenomena. . . .

The reviewer is reminded of an English educator who said to her, of a mass of evidence showing the frequency of neurotic disturbances in early childhood, 'I think your picture is greatly exaggerated. Of course my own children had these troubles, but naturally I took no notice of them.'

Experience has long shown how difficult it is to keep the scientific and didactic points of view apart in these fields of inquiry and how hardly come by is objectivity.

Susan's ability to cover so large an area of editing and review writing in addition to all the other work she was doing for her students and her patients and those who served them, owed much to her capacity for extremely rapid reading and immediate and thorough assimilation of what she read – an ability that many might envy. Her mastery of language had also by then become so much part of herself that it seldom took long for her to find the word or phrase she wanted. On the rare occasions when a word eluded her she would give the question much thought and be full of gratitude if one were able to supply what she was looking for.

As the situation in Europe darkened, political refugees began to come to England considerably before the war and a large part of Susan's time was then devoted to helping them to become established and to find suitable posts. Some of them studied with her and others sought her advice and deeply appreciated her practical and realistic sympathy. Many of the people she helped had worked in the fields of education or clinical psychology and realized how well she understood what they had to offer, which was deeply comforting. She did not often make a mistake in her appraisal of people and would be aware of what was and was not the sphere in which they could best win success or when further training was necessary. If she did make a mistake it would be in over rather than under estimating people, and she would put it right without undermining their confidence if that were in anyway possible. This recalls Flugel's description of her as 'generous and sincere'.

Another sphere of work which took up much of her time was co-operation with all kinds of voluntary societies to which she gave much help. These included the Froebel Society (later the National Froebel Foundation), the Nursery School Association, the Home and School Council, Coram's Fields, play centres and the Foundling Site Training Scheme Committee, the Caldicott Community, the New Education Fellowship, the Save the Children Fund, and many others.

The Institute of Education itself quickly made further use of her services and she was appointed to its Delegacy in 1935. In 1937 they raised her salary from £300 to £325! That was the highest financial recognition she ever received for all she did and even for those days it could not have been described as over-generous! She was driven to having to make a plea for some secretarial help as she could not possibly cover the work involved without increasing the hours of her own private secretary and she had no other.

Apart from official membership on the committees of a great many societies, she gave help also to many others, her realistic and widespread sympathies taking her far afield. She gave a lecture for the Society for Prevention of Accidents which is so full of valuable psychological material about children of all ages that it has since been printed by the journal *Childhood and Youth*. She would give time to such varied causes as helping a group of the clergy who wanted to select and edit material from the Bible which was suited to young children's stage of development; helping a nursery school in danger of being closed because the neighbours disliked the noise of children playing; giving help to those engaged in training nursery nurses; selecting toys and materials for play or working in play centres; and indeed to any cause which came her way, if she felt the happiness and welfare of children was involved. She even went beyond this very wide sphere of interest in people, especially children and their parents, and would support other causes which aroused her ready sympathies as, for example, the humane treatment of animals. If she could not find time to do more than give a donation she was always regretful, but was realistic enough to know that there must be some limitation even to her astonishingly great capacity for work. She gave priority of time to scrupulously careful reading of material on the education and upbringing of children intended for publication, and also to those who wanted to undertake serious research which might lead to the deeper understanding of children, and consequently to their welfare. To cite just one example, she not only responded to a request from the Nursery School Association to consider a long-term investigation into the effects upon children of attending nursery schools, but herself gathered together a group of knowledgeable people, formed a committee, and worked out practicable possibilities which, but for the intervention of war, might well have won financial support and become an actuality. The time devoted to this alone must have been considerable among very many other time-consuming affairs.

As early as 1936, Susan wrote a characteristically generous but firm letter to someone who, in asking for her co-operation, had stated that nothing was being done in England to spread the knowledge of child development. A few paragraphs from this letter show very clearly how widely-spread Susan's activities had become, only three years after the opening of the department.

'Let me start by saying again that I agree with your general aim and policy and admire very greatly the vitality and practical wisdom you have put into it. It is very fortunate that your wide experience and power of seeing all round a question are available at this juncture, and it will be an immense gain if the main elements of your scheme of developing centres all over the country for the help of children who specially need it can be realized. More specifically I welcome your stand on the need to approach the whole question as a problem of growth and the specific study of child development, not as the application of adult psychiatry to children by those who have no first-hand knowledge of childhood. On this point you seem to me entirely

112

right. I like too your plan for establishing these child centres in the different areas of town and country and your general conception of their nature and function, their staffing and their relation to other social and educational services.

'Don't you think, however, that you may be under-estimating the work that is now being done towards the same general aims by other people? I suppose it is possible that you are not aware of everything that is being done, e.g. I feel that the contributions of the Child Guidance Council to preventive mental hygiene and their general educational work of a positive as distinct from a remedial kind do not receive enough recognition in your memo. And the work carried on here at the Institute of Education both in Educational Psychology and Mental Hygiene and in the Department of Child Development is not mentioned. As one example, it seems you did not know all the advisory and research work the Institute has been doing in co-operation with the Wiltshire Education Committee. Possibly you do not know of my own constant collaboration with the Board of Education, with various local education authorities, with many educational bodies such as the New Education Fellowship, the Nursery School Association, Froebel Society, Home and School Council, various training colleges, and other educational associations all over the country, with regard to all the various aspects of child development and of preventive mental hygiene. This is not to mention the regular work of the department in giving experience and training in these fields on an advanced level.

'At the end of your memorandum you emphasize your wish to co-operate with other bodies. Don't you feel that the possibility of co-operation rests upon the acknowledgement of work actually being done by others?

'Of course one cannot acknowledge what one does not know about, but I confess I was troubled to note that in referring to the influences at present at work in child psychology and mental hygiene your memorandum did not at any point refer to my own work. It is of course generally considered, both here and in many parts of the world, that my publications and practical work and teaching have made some contribution to the problems of intellectual growth and social development in the normal child, to preventive mental hygiene in the home and the nursery school, to methods of education and (in my psycho-analytical studies) to the understanding of difficulties of development.

'I do not feel that anyone is obliged to take notice of my work in a general way, but it is a little puzzling that when you seek my active co-operation and wish me to join with you in discussing the present position and considering practical plans, you should not refer to my contributions or the work of this department.'

The letter reveals that Susan was very sympathetic to the work of the child guidance clinics; she found time to co-operate actively with them and they in return welcomed her students as observers and gave appointments to people whom she specially recommended to seek their help. In the early stages of her work in the department, Dr William Moodie's clinic at Islington gave special help to her students and later when other demands on their services became over many, the North Western Clinic under Dr Paterson Brown undertook to give special help to Susan's students. She herself became a vice-president of this clinic in 1933. Other clinics also gave help to her students: these included the Tavistock Clinic, the clinic under Dr Mildred Creak at the Maudesley Hospital, and Dr Winnicott's out-patients' department at the Paddington Green Children's Hospital. Many students found there, as I did, great inspiration from the privilege of watching how sensitively and surely he was able to give the kind of help which was most needed by children and parents under the conditions of an ordinary out-patients' department which most people would have thought were almost impossible for giving any psychological help at all, but which was the only way most of these patients could possibly have obtained it.

In addition to Susan's other work, she continued at least until 1935 in her capacity as Research Assistant at University College and her correspondence shows that she devoted a great deal of time to the supervision of these students. It is also clear that when her health began to give trouble, Professor Cyril Burt was doing his best to reduce the work for her, though missing it very much.

In 1935 the first symptom of cancer, which thirteen years later was to end her life, made its appearance. She underwent an operation in the summer and in December that year she had radium treatment; in January 1936 she suffered what was first taken to be an attack of pleurisy, but later proved to be due to the radium having caused a burn. Her doctors fought devotedly for her and Susan gave the kind of deep understanding and interested co-operation which all those who attended her later were to appreciate. The doctors realized that she was a patient from whom the truth must not be concealed and who would fully justify their confidence. Perhaps her own beginning of a medical training may have played a part in the exceedingly good relationship she always had with doctors and nurses, a relationship based on mutual sympathy and respect. Susan was too realistic not to know and grieve for the gravity of the situation, but she was no defeatist. She had sought medical help directly she suspected trouble. One of her doctors told me that had knowledge at that time been as advanced as it was at the time of her death, it was possible that the trouble might have been permanently ended. Her condition yielded exceedingly well to remedies, but the remedies themselves in the end had too severe an effect and had to be discontinued. That tragedy, however, was still far ahead in 1935. She had to be away from her work for the whole of the spring term and spent most of it in a nursing home, but she made a good recovery and returned to the Institute for the summer term. Sir Percy Nunn was ill at the same time but other colleagues rallied to support her students and Miss Wacey, the Secretary of the Institute, took a special interest in the students and sent reassuring reports to Susan, who was naturally distressed on their behalf since she had no deputy and outside people had to be enlisted to give most of the teaching required. The students played their part in reassuring her and insisted that a good and valuable course had been arranged for them though they naturally rejoiced to see her back for the summer term. Their affection made them very eager to avoid making demands on her. When she left the nursing home in July 1935, Sir Percy Nunn wrote to urge her to take her convalescence seriously and not attempt to hurry it. He wrote: 'Now is the time to cultivate a little of that laziness which is a proper component of human nature, but one you have, I fear, rather scandalously ignored.' She appears to have taken his advice both then and during her second convalescence after the lung trouble.

Once back in her post, however, she assumed very nearly her full programme of activity and in 1937 a further call on her services opened up both a still wider sphere of service and also many new pleasurable interests and personal friendships. She was invited to be one of a team of lecturers for a conference to be held in Australia and New Zealand during July, August, and September.

The conference was arranged by the New Educational Fellowship and the Australian Council for Educational Research with the co-operation of the New Zealand Council. The team travelled out via America and spent a short time there, and Susan formed personal friendships in that country with many people whose published work she had greatly respected. Her files contain letters from many American friends, some of whom later visited her in England: among them Barbara Burks, Sidone Gruenberg, Louisa Wagoner, Rose Alschuler, Gardner and Lois Barclay Murphy, and many others – including Katherine Bridges in Canada. She had only two days in New York, largely filled with engagements made with her by the Child Study Association, but she also visited other parts of the United States including California where she was able to see the work of Jean Walker MacFarlane at Berkley College which she had always greatly admired. This was a longitudinal study of children whose parents also gave data. Susan was impressed by the amount and nature of the wishes, fears, and anxieties of children and parents which Dr MacFarlane's research 'subjects' were prepared to confide, and which she said she would not have thought possible outside a clinical relationship. She did not seem aware that many of her own personal friends were often willing to confide as fully in her, though she did not overlook the fact that Jean Mac-Farlane's subjects had also become her friends.

The party divided after leaving America and some of them, including Susan, stopped in New Zealand and went on to Australia later. Susan's lectures were given mainly in Auckland and Wellington, but she certainly visited Christchurch and probably other cities. For the conference, speakers divided between the North and South Islands, but they broadcast certain talks both in New Zealand and in Australia. Memories of Susan's contributions are still very vivid in the minds of many Australians and New Zealanders. She created a tremendous impression and spoke to crowded audiences of people who had often come long distances to hear her and waited early in the morning to secure places in the halls in which she spoke. Arnold Campbell, recently Director of Education for New Zealand, got to know her very well, as did his predecessor Dr C. E. Beeby who at the time of Susan's visit there was Director of the New Zealand Council for Educational Research. Mr Campbell had been interested in Susan since the publication of her criticism of Piaget in 1925. He said the nursery and infant teachers in New Zealand were very quick to realize the importance of her work, and that her writings had made her name a very respected one long before 1937, though at that date the education given to young children was still rather formal and only a few people held more liberal views. He explained that, although the economic depression had hit New Zealand very hard, a sense of change was in the air for which he ascribed credit to Mr Peter Frazer, a vigorous Minister of Education, and afterwards New Zealand's second Labour Prime Minister. Susan came into this 'Revivalist atmosphere' and spoke with authority. Arnold Campbell himself had a deep respect for her. He spoke of the great impact of her lectures and the handling of the many questions which were put to her, which he said was *beautifully* done'. She never met a hostile question with hostility but treated it seriously, always offering clear and impressive evidence for what she had said so that hostility melted and discussion became constructive.

Arnold Campbell described her as a sensitive and rather shy person and very conscientious. He said it was characteristic of her that she left all her notes in beautiful order, which eased his work on reporting the conference. It was also characteristic of her courtesy and concern for people that she made every possible effort to enable people to hear her at one lecture when the loud speaker broke down.

He considered her as an 'immensely wise woman' and also as 'one of nature's intellectuals', and said that she was intensely curious about many things and always sought for further understanding. Among other matters she was extremely interested in New Zealand's speech conventions such as 'fossick about',[1] and would pursue the question of their origins.

As in America, so in Australia and New Zealand, Susan made many friends with whom she kept up the contact in later years. In Australia she was specially assigned to the south for most of her tour, but went long distances to lecture. She lectured in Brisbane, Sydney, Melbourne, Perth, Adelaide, and Hobart. Everywhere she met with the warmest of receptions and made an abiding contribution, especially to the education of young children. The University of Adelaide awarded her the honorary degree of Doctor of Science. Her files contain a wealth of correspondence with Australian educationists, and many of them visited her later in England. One Australian college sent comforts for her to distribute to nursery schools during the war years and continued this kindness till the end of the war, as well as sending personal gifts to her at times of her illnesses. Both Australia and New Zealand sought her help in filling leading appointments and gave a kindly welcome to people to whom she gave introductions when they wished to made their future in these countries. She wanted me to go to Adelaide as principal of their Kindergarten Training College, because at that time they had asked her to find someone from England for that post,

[1] English equivalent is 'rummage about'.

118

and had it not been for the outbreak of war I should probably have done so. At a later stage I was glad to know their wish to have this link with us had been granted in the appointment of Miss Margaret Roberts, who is now my successor in the Department of Child Development, and had herself also a link with Susan Isaacs. This would have given Susan great pleasure. Deeply as she respected the contribution of the U.S.A., she felt a great wish to accede to the request of one of the Kindergarten Colleges to have a strong connection for some few years with this country, and at that time when Australia wished to add an influence from outside, it was nearly always easier to find someone available from the U.S.A. than from England.

Susan's new friendships also, of course, included fellow members of the team who worked together and very much enjoyed each other's stimulating company. The members of the Overseas Delegation who travelled out for the conference were:

WILLIAM BOYD, M.A., B.SC., D.Phil., Head of Department of Education, University of Glasgow.

PIERRE BOVET, Docteur es lettres (Geneva), HON.Litt.D., Director J. J. Rousseau Institute for Educational Sciences, Geneva.

EDMUND DE S. BRUNNER, M.A., Ph.D., B.D., Professor of Education, Columbia University, New York.

W. SALTER DAVIES, C.B.E., M.A., Director of Education, Kent.

F. DEBENHAM, O.B.E., M.A., Professor of Geography, University of Cambridge.

PAUL L. DENGLER, Ph.D., Head of Austro-American Institute, Vienna.

MRS BEATRICE ENSOR, President and Organizing Director, New Education Fellowship.

F. W. HART, Ph.D., Professor of Education, University of California.

H. R. HAMLEY, M.A., M.SC., Ph.D., Professor of Education, University of London.

F. C. HAPPOLD, D.S.O., M.A., Headmaster, Bishop Words-
worth's School, Salisbury, England.

G. T. HANKIN, B.A., Representative of Board of Education,
England.

DR SUSAN ISAACS, M.A., D.SC., University of London, Institute of Education.

I. L. KANDEL, M.A., Ph.D., Professor of Education,
Teachers' College, Columbia University, New York.

A. LISMER, A.R.C.A., Educational Supervisor, Art Gallery,
Toronto, Canada.

E. G. MALHERBE, M.A., Ph.D., Director, National Bureau
of Educational and Social Research, Pretoria, South Africa.

SIR PERCY MEADON, C.B.E., M.A., Director of Education,
Lancashire, England.

CYRIL NORWOOD, M.A., D.Litt., President, St John's
College, Oxford.

HAROLD RUGG, C.E., Ph.D., Ped.D., Professor of Education, Teachers' College, Columbia Univeristy, New York.

YUSUKE TSURUMI, M.P., Representative, Japan.

ANDERS VEDEL (Degrees from University of Copenhagen),
Principal, Krabbesholm Folk High School, Jutland.

LAURIN ZILLIACUS, B.SC., Tolo Svenska Samsola, Helsing-
fors, Finland.

Susan enjoyed the lighter side of the trip, and with her usual
sense of fun, rejoiced in the amusing incidents which occurred.
She related an episode after a ceremonial banquet given to the
team in Fiji, when after dinner a choir of magnificent men, looking like warriors prepared for war, strode forward to sing. When
they opened their mouths to sing she held her breath, waiting
for a stupendous experience – instead of which the audience was
offered, as a compliment to the English visitors, two children's
songs 'Oh dear, what can the matter be' followed by 'Baa baa,
black sheep'. After that they did give a concert of their own
music and she was much impressed, but was regretful that their
idea of English or European music was evidently gained from

their early school-days! She was also delighted by a flurried chairman in New Zealand who introduced her as 'Dr Isan Susaacs', and by the indignation of her admirers when a local paper described her as 'a little handful of femininity'.

Her letters refer to the gracious hospitality they received in all three countries and also show how much she enjoyed the whole experience. To Grace Owen she wrote, 'I had a wonderful tour, and was immensely interested in all the various aspects of the work being done for young children in America, New Zealand, and Australia. . . . It is, of course, very pleasant to be home again, but the tour was immensely stimulating and interesting.'

Susan returned to even fuller activity in the department because the tour had brought her still more personal contacts, professional inquiries, and requests for advice from visitors sent to her by people she had met on the tour. By this time she had further added to her teaching commitments by undertaking the course in normal child psychology given at the London School of Economics to those training to be psychiatric social workers. Their tutor, Miss Sybil Clement Brown, who had admitted Susan's students to her own lectures in sociology, had been a friend of Susan's since 1929 and used to attend meetings of the Aristotelian Society and the British Psychological Society with Susan and Nathan. She was one of a circle which met for social evenings in Susan's home every week-end. Discussion was lively and wit sparkling. Miss Clement Brown said she was impressed by Susan's 'lightning mind' – when she joined in the discussion she went straight from one idea to the next without any tortuous route to get there. She said both mind and body were quite unusually quick, and her home a place of gracious hospitality. Good meals and beautiful flowers were always available and the gatherings 'intellectually warming and worth while on every level'. As a teacher of the mental health course students, she described Susan as very imaginative and lively – but sometimes inclined to leap on to psycho-analytic interpretation without the evidence she would have considered essential in other matters. Miss Clement Brown thought she was perhaps less critical of ideas from that field of study, which meant so much to her, than she would have been of evidence from other sources. It is possible that this was partly due to the severe time-limit imposed by a course of only twelve lectures on the whole of child and adolescent development, together with the methods of studying children. When I later took this course over from Susan I became very conscious of this problem. Susan's papers on 'Criteria of Interpretation', published in her last book, *Childhood and After*, show that she was quite capable of looking at evidence in the field of psycho-analysis, but it may well be that in economizing time, she sometimes overlooked the fact that certain material which now seemed self-evident to her from her clinical experience would not be equally so to her audience.

During 1937, plans for moving the Institute of Education into its new building in the Senate House of the University of London were afoot. Sir Fred Clarke wrote in a report of the Institute Bulletin: 'The greater space available for the work of the department in the new building has brought new possibilities of work. In the old building all activities of the department, with the exception of the main lecture courses, were carried on in the one room: the students' reading, tutorial work and seminars, conferences with teachers, advising of parents and teachers, testing children, interviews with workers in child guidance and child welfare, and with visitors from America and the Dominions. Now we have expanded into three rooms. Dr Isaacs' own office, with its fine west window, is a delightful place in which to receive distinguished visitors and fellow workers and to hold small conferences. The students have a reading-room of their own, where smaller seminars can also be held and the library of the department expanded to something more adequate to the needs of the students. The third room has made possible an important advance in the work of the department, namely, the establishment of a nursery play group for six or seven children between two and five years of age, in daily attendance. This has been delightfully fitted up and is in itself a cheering sight in an Institute of Education. The children also have the use of the roof, which later on it is hoped to turn into a garden and play-ground. The care of the play group is in the hands of Miss Pamela Norman, herself a former pupil of Dr Isaacs in the Malting House School, Cambridge, who has been trained for nursery school work at the Rachel MacMillan College. During the present term Miss D. E. May, who was last year the holder of the Leon Bequest Fellowship for an investigation into the social development of young children, formerly Superintendent of Somers Town Nursery School, has very kindly consented to act as tutor and to give Miss Norman the benefit of her unusual experience and wisdom with regard to the education of young children. The purpose of the play group is to provide students with the chance of seeing ordinary healthy young children in happy play, as well as to give life and reality to the teaching of child development. The number of students in the Department this year has almost over-stepped even the new accommodation.' Susan had the work of planning the playroom and ordering furniture. The equipment for the playroom was largely supplied by the generosity of her old friend Paul Abbatt, whose father had so kindly received the six-year-old Susan, in the long ago days in Bolton, when she ran away from home and announced that she wished to be his wife!

When the department moved into its new premises in the autumn of 1938, it seemed that high hopes of expansion were at last about to be realized. The number of students, despite severe restriction, was already twenty, too many for a full-time tutor, and Susan's was never more than a half-time appointment. The rest of her time was fully occupied with clinical work and with the affairs of the psycho-analytic society during a period of controversy when she did a great deal to help and support the work of Melanie Klein. She was making realistic and carefully considered appeals for more staff for the Department of Child Development when the shadow of war which had, of course, threatened for a long time, became a stark reality.

Susan left the Senate House building for the summer vacation of 1939, never to return.

A very clear indication of how widely her activities were ranging before the intervention of the war can be seen in her report made in February 1939 at the request of the director (see Appendix II).

6 · The last nine years

As to all sensitive people, the outbreak of war was inexpressibly distressing to Susan. The threat of it had often been the subject of the week-end discussions in her home, but up to the last she had not wholly abandoned hope. Her nature was never to indulge in pessimism though neither, of course, in a thoughtless and superficial optimism. The ordeal of war was to reveal once more her superb ability to overcome difficulties and never accept defeat, but rather seek to extract from a tragic situation opportunities for giving constructive help to children. Perhaps her willingness to admit the first feelings of utter depression played its part in enabling her to recover her poise so well and so soon. She said to me before the war that if it occurred, 'Everything which you and I stand for may be lost', and her early feelings are revealed in a letter which she wrote to her friend Mr George Lyward to whom she had promised an article which she had not had the heart to write. It is dated 27th October 1939.

Dear Mr Lyward,

I am a pig! And I'm awfully sorry about it. But I have something under way, if you can wait a few days – on evacuation problems.

I have wanted to write something, but it seems to be writing in particular which has got inhibited by the upheaval of the war. It will come back, and is beginning to. But it seemed as if I could feel only *personal* relationships to be valuable for a time, in direct contact, not through the medium of writing.

There have been a great many practical urgencies, too. We are starting a systematic survey of evacuation problems here in

Cambridge – with the help of L.S.E., Bedford College and Cambridge experts. And I am one of the conveners. This has meant a lot of letters and meetings, etc.

It was quite extraordinary to me, however, how *writing* about problems (to which so much of my life hitherto has been devoted) suddenly became unreal and worthless.

However, it is coming to life again. Can you wait a few days? I hop to finish some pages over the week-end.

With deep apologies,

Ever yours,
SUSAN ISAACS

I admired the last number very much – how *do* you get so much interesting and valuable stuff together?

N.B. Having *no* secretarial help has of course contributed largely to the slowing down of my output. I'm glad to say that I'm getting my secretary back, part-part-time, on Monday.'

This letter reveals how quickly Susan was turning her mind to the problems of children, indeed she had offered her help in the evacuation of London children. For a time it seemed probable that the Department of Child Development would continue to function and Susan was involved in plans for this. The Senate House building was taken over by the Ministry of Information and the Institute of Education went to Nottingham. At first Sir Fred Clarke proposed to have the department there if Susan could manage to be in Nottingham for certain days each week. At one stage it seemed more appropriate to keep it in some other building in London and finally the attempt to re-open it was abandoned, since English teachers would not be released for full-time study and it was highly improbable that overseas students would be able to travel, even if they wished to take the risk of doing so. Quite a number of students would have been available immediately and had to be put off, but there was little prospect of the supply of candidates being maintained. Susan herself suggested, with her characteristic generosity, that since other colleagues might find their work cut down and have difficulty in finding suitable posts, whereas she had another way of supporting herself, she should forego her salary and go into full-time clinical work. Before doing this, however, she made the only offer she was ever to make, to give up her clinical work altogether for the duration of the war. She felt that, at a time of such tragedy, she ought to offer her help to more children, so she wrote to the Board of Education and offered her services if she should be needed. This letter never reached the higher levels of the Board and merely received a formal acknowledgement – probably from some junior clerk who was unaware of what this offer meant. Later on when, too late, the higher authorities learnt that she had offered her services they were horrified that the opportunity had been lost and were convinced that the Ministry of Health, in conjunction with them, would have been most willing to entrust the whole training of personnel for the war-time nurseries to her direction; thus many of the early mistakes would have been avoided, to the tremendous benefit of large numbers of children. Susan herself assumed that her services would not be required and went back to her clinical work. She retained the nominal headship of the Department of Child Development and coped with its extensive correspondence in an unpaid capacity.

However, it was not long before opportunities for public service to children came her way. Her friend Miss Clement Brown suggested she should move to Cambridge where she herself would be going because the London School of Economics was being moved there. The idea appealed to Susan since it meant that she could continue with certain patients who were going there, as well as going on with her course for the Mental Health students. Moreover, Nathan's firm, which was of great importance to the war effort, was moving into Warwickshire and she felt the journey from Cambridge would not be too difficult for her to be able to join him at week-ends. Susan astonished Miss Clement Brown by the rapidity with which she acted on her suggestion. She went straight down to Cambridge, found a flat and invited Clement to come and share it with her, which offer was gladly accepted. Susan invited me to stay with her there very shortly after she had moved in and I shall always remember that visit with gratitude as it gave me, for the first time since the outbreak of war, the feeling that life was still worth while. It was less than a month after the outbreak of war, so the memory of that visit recalls to me again how swiftly she could pass from her own sorrow to comfort and support others. She took me to see the Malting House School building which we had to look at through chinks in a fence. We discussed many things including, of course, education and the needs of children in war time. She was delighted that I was not proposing to give up my research into the effects upon children of progressive as compared with formal education, but that I was going to spend October in gathering the children from Leeds and the villages to which they had moved out, in order to give the final tests before the Leeds Training College where I was working re-opened on 1st November in Scarborough.

One evening she asked me if I would go on the river with her and proposed to take a canoe. On the way she remarked casually, 'You can swim can't you?' and when I assented said, 'Then if it turns over you'll be able to save me.' I had never before forced my will against Susan's inclinations but on hearing that she herself could *not* swim, I absolutely insisted on a boat with oars and said I refused to risk the terrible responsibility of possibly drowning her! When I later said I hoped this less exciting method of river travel had not spoilt her pleasure too much, she said, with a twinkle in her eye, 'Not at all. Thank you for saving my life,' and told me of a small girl who in a composition on pins had written, 'Pins have saved a great many lives.' When her teacher asked, 'How have they saved lives?' the child had replied, 'By not swallowing them.' So Susan felt I could claim a like credit for not drowning her! Her sense of fun was evident on several occasions during this short visit and her zest for life had returned to her without, of course, the need to deny her feelings of sadness. While we were enjoying the lovely view of the Cambridge Backs, she said how terrible the loss to humanity would be if so much beauty were destroyed.

All through the war Susan, while fully recognizing its implication and danger, showed herself able to bring to bear on it both her robust common sense and her interest in the psychological effects which it produced upon herself and others. One evening, later, when she was back in London and I called for her on a night of air raids, because she was to give a lecture for us, I said, 'I feel dreadful to bring you out on a night like this.' She replied, 'How do you know that you are not saving my life? My flat might be hit while I am out,' and she went on to speak with interest about the illusion we all had that we were safer inside and how hard we should find it to follow the official instructions to get out into the open rather than back into a bus if explosives were falling when we were about to alight. She was also amused and interested at the relatively gay, though mildly indignant, attitude of people when they met on Primrose Hill to view the first flying bombs, compared with their much more sober behaviour when meeting there on V.E. night, after a day of anxiously waiting for the news. She was also well aware of, and able to share, the reluctance of people to go away from London leaving loved people behind, while they did not worry about those same people when they were at home too – 'as if one's mere presence could protect them'. Nathan once consented to sleep at my home in Surrey and travel to London daily in order to allow Susan to take a much needed holiday with a mind at greater ease about him.

Very soon after settling in Cambridge, Susan became involved in a research into the problems of evacuation both for children and their temporary foster parents. This was just the kind of constructive work for children which she was so eager to extract from the tragedy of war ('turning disaster into use' as Miss Clement Brown put it). Not only was this survey of value to children in the contemporary situation, but it enabled Susan later to give most impressive evidence to the Curtis committee on the care of children deprived of normal home life. Clement said the work began a year after the war and of course it entailed much preliminary planning. Students who were in training as social workers at the London School of Economics were able to assist with collecting data but the whole question of obtaining evidence both from foster parents and children was a very delicate one calling for great discernment, sympathy, and wisdom. Susan was chairman of the committee for the research and had access to a team of distinguished and knowledgeable people, including Dr Thouless and Miss Margery Fry. Dr John Bowlby was also in Cambridge till he joined the army; he was always a friend to Susan and she had a great regard for him and his work. Herbert Read also visited her there. The Canonbury Child Guidance Clinic was in Cambridge for part of the time and Susan already had contacts there. Miss Clement Brown said that Susan worked terrifically hard to get the evidence and was eager to counteract the idea that everything was bad. She felt there were great opportunities available to many people in the evacuation – including the teachers, and she helped to form a social club for those who were feeling isolated. She was certain that this survey was very well worth doing – she did not hold a meticulously severe view of the need for rigid methods of taking evidence but said that the sincerely held opinions of teachers were well worth gathering and that even less precisely taken evidence would get them nearer the truth than anything else they could get at that stage on that problem. This was typical of her realistic common sense. She said to me that despite the widespread publicity given to the failures, it was heartening to find in how many cases happy relationships were established between children and their temporary foster parents, but that the adolescents were the most difficult to settle happily. The full work is published in the book *The Cambridge Evacuation Survey* (Methuen) which she put together and edited. By September 1940 the writing up of material had begun; that was at the time of the Battle of Britain. Clement recalls how the morning after the City of London was on fire, she felt she must go up to London, but Susan felt they would be much more useful if they went on writing up the survey. It had reached a critical stage: Susan said one crisis should not be put off by another and Clement felt she had kept her perspective. When the book was published, *The Times* gave it very good publicity and it was widely read by those concerned with the evacuation of children.

During Susan's time in Cambridge, Melanie Klein lived with her and Clement Brown for about a year, after which Susan felt it was too dangerous a place for so valuable a person and persuaded her to make her home somewhere more remote from the peril of air raids. Mrs Klein was impressed by Susan's competence in domestic matters as well as in so many others. Clement said that both Mrs Klein and Susan had such a gift for remembering every detail about their patients that they never needed to write notes after an interview and that, if time between appointments permitted, Susan would go out to gather or buy flowers, for which she had a passion, or do shopping or get her hair done. She certainly packed a great deal into her life and was an adept at not wasting the odd ten minutes. I have known her use such an interval for adding a paragraph or two to a book or article. She could also relax equally quickly and, if needed, could use the ten minutes for a refreshing nap. This ability probably explains why on the whole (though not entirely) she maintained her health through this period when, in addition to working very hard, she had a most awkward journey involving cycling and two changes of trains, when she met Nathan at week-ends, and a certain number of journeys to Nottingham where she gave some lectures to the Institute of Education postgraduate students.

She gave up the flat later as the owner wished to return and she then lived in a house in Cambridge. In 1943 she returned to her London flat and, as always, wherever she was living, planned and cultivated a garden once more.

In 1943 she was urged by some inspectors of the Ministry of Education to try to get the Department of Child Development opened again. They were aware that as soon as hostilities ceased, there would be an urgent need to train many teachers in emergency colleges, and that during the war there had been no opportunity for gifted teachers to carry their studies further and so fit them for posts as lecturers in these colleges. Susan consulted Sir Fred Clarke and proposed that if he agreed to re-open, she would retain her contact by taking the main course of lectures as an honorary lecturer if he would allow the salary to be used for someone of her choice to be in charge of the department and conduct the other courses. When he agreed she did me the honour of inviting me, but was concerned that I should not have to lose a full-time salary by taking up what was then still her part-time post. She suggested another part-time appointment for me, but deeply as I longed to work with her, I was worried about the possibility of not doing justice to the Department in view of the fact that the other post, though interesting, would inevitably be a very demanding one. So I asked her whether Sir Fred Clarke might not feel that the time was ripe for making a full-time appointment for the Department of Child Development since it must inevitably expand very rapidly as soon as the war ended. Susan felt I was right about this and Sir Fred did also, but he said the post would then have to be advertised in the usual way unless Susan herself would have been willing to stay on. She, however, insisted on resigning. Once more her determination to remain in clinical work was something so strong that nothing could move her, neither Nathan's 'eloquent and forcible persuasions' nor the fact that those she most admired in the field of psycho-analysis added their advice to his.

The psycho-analysts felt that though she was a good analyst, there were others in that field, whereas in her position as head of the Department of Child Development at the University of London, she would be in a unique position to build the bridge between their work and that of education. The educationalists added their efforts of persuasion and I was implored to add mine, which indeed I longed as much as any to do, but I felt that she had the right to make her own decision and, in any case, I should have had no more hope of success than the rest. I therefore re-frained, except for letting her know how pleased we should all be if she did so decide. I felt very troubled that my own action had lost her generous offer to the department, but she scouted this idea and when I was appointed was deeply and sincerely delighted. Though she would not take the main lectures course because she said she did not want to give anyone the excuse for saying that I had had to turn to her for this, she offered to give a course on the influence of psycho-analysis upon education which she said no one could expect me to do. She continued to give this course of ten lectures for the department until only a year before her death. By the time I was appointed in September 1943, Susan was in process of moving back to London. She was staying in her London flat at the time of the meeting of the committee which was to make the appointment and asked me to spend the night with her, as she said, 'I'd like to have you with me whether you get it or whether you don't.' When I said, 'I'd like to be with you, especially if I don't,' she replied, 'I thought of that too!' No one could ever wish for a more sympathetic or supporting predecessor and though I inevitably had considerable anxieties about the impossibility of living up to her standards, this was an idea I would not have dared to express to her! When on one occasion, I revealed some such feeling, by an inadvertently vehement assent to her saying of someone else, 'One *could* understand, I suppose, how a person could feel like that?', it brought me a five-page letter the next day about the absurdity of getting such an idea, emphasizing, in most generous terms, what I could give the department and ending the letter with, 'So no more of that nonsense, damn you!' says she in her polite way of writing to her friends.

Susan lent me her flat during November when I came to London as she was using it only for week-ends, so I met her on Friday evenings each week and soon after Christmas she was finally established in London again. Her time as usual was very fully occupied with patients and with the affairs of the psycho-analytic society but she found time to help me a great deal in the preliminary work of getting the department launched again and the Chelsea Nursery School re-opened. She came to a committee I had invited to advise me on what research could most usefully be undertaken by the department during the war and advised me who else I might invite, including John Bowlby. One of Susan's suggestions was that we should never again have as good a chance of finding out whether it had caused any permanent handicap to children if they had not learned to read before the age of nine, because so many London schools had, during the war, been obliged to exclude the younger children owing to lack of space. Unfortunately the department at the Ministry of Education which controlled the release of teachers was not in touch with those who had urged the department to re-open and I found I could have no full-time students till some time after the war ended. The research ideas could not be implemented when I had to run the department on a part-time basis with all classes given in the evenings, and the only investigations my students could undertake were somewhat limited topics which were feasible to carry out with their own children and which Susan herself never felt could be wholly satisfactory when done by those who had to teach at the same time. My own day-time hours were quickly filled by attempting to keep pace with Susan's legacy of committee and advisory work, not to mention such practical tasks as trying to acquire furniture for the department and also for the Chelsea Nursery School whose trustees had generously given everything to the war-time nurseries and were, by then, unable to get permits to buy anything, since it was not a war-time nursery! Susan contributed some furniture from her own flat and reassured Miss Grove, the newly appointed head of the school (another of her old students), when people criticized. The first children to be admitted were often those who had been gravely disturbed by the war; as soon as they were becoming stable it was time for them to leave and we acquired other distressed children. Susan said, 'It doesn't really do to worry about what people say! I always found, at the Malting House, that if visitors came on a good day they said, "Of course these methods are all right with such *easy* children", but if it was a bad day, they said, "You see what these awful methods lead to".' I knew she was very busy and her health was by no means good so I refrained from asking her too much for advice but it was, of course, the greatest comfort and support to be able to turn to her in matters of real perplexity. Though she never offered advice she gave it generously any time I asked for it. She also enjoyed hearing about the affairs of the department and could always see and enjoy the funny side of certain things that happened. I felt very relaxed and able to talk freely to her without fear of tiring her for I was aware that it gave her pleasure. She never lost interest in the department though her time was given mainly to psycho-analysis.

She rejoiced in her appointment as a training analyst and devoted much time and concentration to this work and to the affairs of the society. Dr Paula Heimann, who had known her since 1933, told me that she and Susan sometimes wrote papers together and were often asked to present Mrs Klein's views on various subjects to the Psycho-analytic Society. She said that on one occasion, when writing a paper on 'Regression' together they came to a point where they 'dried up'. Susan went to the piano and played Bach, whose music they both loved, and Dr Heimann said how appropriate his name, meaning 'brook', was. As she listened she said she felt 'life coming back with the brook' and she began to write while Susan offered to go on playing if it helped. Susan herself was masterly in her presentation of Mrs Klein's work but would not write at her dictation. She took the points and wrote afterwards.

Dr Heimann was impressed by Nathan's and Susan's double desk and the concentrated way they wrote their own work from opposite sides of it – an indication of the rich relationship between them. She felt that Susan made a great contribution by her wide knowledge and the great clarity of her mind when she was going into a subject or presenting a problem in very great detail. She never just expressed 'hunches' but went to tremendous pains to give the full picture. Dr Heimann said that Susan could conceptualize and verbalize Mrs Klein's 'hunches' and Mrs Klein relied on her very much for this. Mrs Klein was a frequent visitor to Susan's home and felt gratitude and admiration for Susan when she carried on with writing the regression paper both before and after undergoing a severe operation. In 1946 Susan broke it to me that she had to have this operation and then did her best to cheer me, asking if I would visit her in the nursing home and then turning the subject off to question me with genuine interest about the affairs of the department. She objected strongly to people telling her she had courage but it is not at all surprising that people did so. Her last two years were a gallant and constant struggle against ill health, not merely from the cancer and the distressing symptoms caused by the remedies, for in late 1947 she also had to have an operation for a duodenal ulcer. Between her illnesses she worked unremittingly, but also found time for her friends. It was during these last years (in August 1947) that she presented her evidence to the Curtis Committee in person as well as submitting a memorandum which is published in her book, *Childhood and After*. She showed me a list she had drawn up of points to observe when visiting a children's home and asked me to add my points, if I had any, to her own. She was pleased when I suggested noticing whether the toys looked as if they had been used or were in too beautiful a condition!

I saw a great deal of her during her last five years from 1943–1948 and was impressed with the way, when not interrupted by illness, she kept a balance between her main preoccupation with patients and psycho-analytic work, while giving much help still to education by contributing articles, giving Press interviews, writing advice to teachers and parents who consulted her, and even sometimes giving lectures. It was not until January 1946 that she finally gave up her course for the London School of Economics, though I had attended her lectures in the previous autumn in order to take over at short notice if ill health required her to miss a lecture or break off the course. She took her course for my department in the summer of 1946 for the last time and I remember her grief in having to give it up after that. It was fortunate that the maisonette which I rented had a large room on the first floor in which I assembled all the chairs I possessed and some students sat on the floor on cushions. The very short distance between my home and hers was the reason she was able to carry on so long with this course. The first evening she lectured there, the electric lights had just expired all over the house and I can still remember how beautiful and impressive she looked in that Regency period room lighted only by candles, one on each side of the table at which she sat to give her lecture. I admitted a great many people besides my own students, as so many were eager for this opportunity of hearing her.

Another balance she maintained was between work and leisure and the time she reserved for her friends, and for many young relatives and their friends. She had a very warm affection for Nathan's niece Karina who had often stayed with her in Cambridge and Warwickshire. On one of her later birthdays when Nathan asked what she would like for a celebration she asked him to take her somewhere where she could watch young people dancing. Though she loved the theatre she found in these later years, when her full-time clinical work involved her in the need to do so much concentrated listening, that she preferred forms of entertainment which appealed to the eye rather than the ear unless of course it was music, which she always loved and would play to herself when alone. She enjoyed the ballet and the circus too, being convinced that by those days the animals were trained humanely. She found the trust of the acrobatic performers in each other a moving and inspiring thing and always appreciated physical skill and grace. She would also enjoy a silent film. Nathan had taught her chess and she was a keen player. In moods when she wanted to relax she liked to read detective stories and had a special admiration for those of Agatha Christie. She enjoyed straightforward fiction which told a good story, presented realistic people, and avoided the supernatural; she disliked ill-digested psychology, which irritated her intensely.

Travelling opportunities were limited by her unwillingness to break the regular appointments of her patients, but in September 1943 she had attended a dinner given in honour of illustrious women who had been students of Manchester. Most of those invited had refused, catering in war-time was difficult, and the students who had organized the affair were full of apprehension, but Susan's charm completely captivated them and they felt she had made the occasion a shining success. She too very much enjoyed it. It was characteristic of her that she never forgot those who had contributed to her work. At the last public lecture she ever gave in the summer of 1946 she paid a very warm tribute to Grace Owen; and if she could possibly accede to a request for her services from her native town of Bolton and her first University of Manchester she would always do so. When I wrote to Miss Owen about this, she replied:

'I was very moved by what you wrote me of S. Isaacs' generous tribute to the inspiration that came to her through me years ago – and no less by your goodness in writing to tell me. . . .

'It is wonderful to me to have had the privilege of having S. Isaacs in my group when she began preparing for her educational career. But perhaps what I am most glad of, is to have been able to take a hand in persuading her to enter the more advanced courses which were obviously calling her. I am very proud of her work.'

Susan continued to take holidays, always if possible, seeking the mountains of Switzerland or the highlands of Scotland. When she could have a week-end out of London she would choose somewhere like Hindhead where she could enjoy high and hilly country.

By 1947 she was well aware that her life could not be preserved for very much longer and she was anxious to use her time for publishing any material which might help people. She once said, 'It seems such a waste to have to go when I could be helping people.' For that reason and because of her great love of Nathan she never accepted defeat and would undergo treatments even when hope of success was not great, and she felt almost too tired to make the further effort. She continued to give the fullest co-operation to her doctors and to respect their knowledge and skill. Moreover she was interested in the reasons for treatments and the psychological effect of a drug which she said she did not like – but it was so interesting that, if well enough, she would like to write a paper on it!

Her two last books embodied much of the material she was most anxious to publish, and I regret that both are now out of print. One is the collection of papers gathered into the book *Childhood and After* (Routledge). Because of lack of time she put into one volume both simple material suited to parents and teachers, and very clinical papers which would appeal to a very different type of reader, and it may well be that is why, when her other books have run into many editions, this one did not. I should very much like to add other valuable educational papers from her files and publish these as a separate book, and it is also possible that someone in the clinical field might care to review her clinical papers. She certainly had not time to use all that was valuable. Her last book *Troubles of Children and Parents* (Methuen) is a selection of letters written for the *Nursery World*, and here also I feel there is a very strong case for publishing some of these again with additions from many helpful and illuminating un-published letters of hers which are in my possession. The prob-lems of young children do not become outdated and many of these letters would still be very helpful to modern parents. Her last piece of writing was her article for the *Journal of Psycho-Analysis* on 'The Nature and Function of Phantasy', which is still the recommended reading on the subject for students train-ing as psycho-analysts. It is reprinted in Volume 43 *Developments in Psycho-Analysis*, published by the Hogarth Press. Nathan's niece, Karina, helped her prepare this for publication.

In January 1948 Susan received the award of the C.B.E. This gave much happiness to Nathan and to her many friends and admirers in this country and in other countries all over the world, and it brought her many letters which could not fail to give her pleasure. Though there was poignancy too in that this recogni-tion was something we knew she could not live long to enjoy, it was a comfort to her friends to have such an opportunity of expressing to her what she and her work had meant to us all. She was not well enough to attend the Investiture, but she held a small gathering of close friends in her flat. They went into her room in twos and threes, while a few of her friends including Evelyn Lawrence and myself, entertained those awaiting their turn to go to her.

She died on the twelfth of October 1948, devotedly tended to the end by Nathan and her doctor and nurses. I was able to be with her on the last day and have always felt there was something very significant in her last words to me; though they arose from a quite trivial incident, they were said with deep conviction as if it were important that I should remember them, 'I like to understand.' To the end she tried to comfort and support her friends in their impending loss and even apologized to me for bringing this sorrow on me. Nor did her sense of humour desert her. She related to me with great delight how her friend Dr Flora Shepherd had replied to a playfully poignant remark of hers, 'I feel it will be so dull in Heaven': 'Oh no, my dear, we shan't be dull at all, because, don't you know, it is there that we shall be able to do research on the long-term effects of congenital mal-formations?' Her thoughts were, of course, most deeply with Nathan; she often spoke of his devoted care of her and concern for giving her every possible comfort and happiness and though he refrained from pressing her, she tried a final form of treatment because she knew he really longed for her to do so. She thought much about his loneliness when she left him and said to him that she wondered whether one day he and their very dear friend Evelyn Lawrence might be able to comfort each other. That hope was eventually fulfilled.

Nathan was comforted to find after the funeral that Mr Peter Fraser, Prime Minister of New Zealand, who was in London at the time, had slipped in unobtrusively among us. Nathan felt that the honour he did to her memory by his presence that day was a fitting sign that the memory of her life and work would be treasured beyond this country. Later, Mr Fraser himself launched a national appeal in New Zealand to support the memorial to her, to endow a fellowship in her name for research in the education of children, thus expressing, to use Nathan's words, 'her two great passions – to understand and to help'.

Among the tributes which poured in from letters of sympathy to Nathan, there is one which for me perhaps expresses best my own feelings about her. Sir Fred Clarke wrote:

'There was that in the sweetness of her presence which reduced one's own troubles to their correct proportions and restored one's hope and confidence. It is that, quite as much as her great achievements, for which she will be remembered with lasting thankfulness and affection. She has achieved great things which will live on and grow, and thousands who have never known her will be the happier for what she has done. . . . It was an immense achievement to prove, as she did, that a strict scientific temper can co-exist with such womanly sweetness and charm.'

Her funeral is described in a letter which brings vividly to remembrance the Susan her friends knew. It was written to *The New Statesman* by Joseph Pole, an old friend of Susan and Nathan, and father of two of the Malting House boys.

'. . . Susan Isaacs was an exciting person to know. Her intellectual vitality enriched a nature boundlessly eager to participate in the adventure of living, and to be counted among her friends was to be admitted to the intimacy of a rare enlightenment that included ruthlessly frank discussion that might range from her own special field of psycho-analysis through literature and politics to the uproarious enjoyment of a "This England", or the recollections of a climbing holiday. Almost the last words that she spoke to the writer a few days before she died were a wryly-humorous reference to the finality of her journey.

'Her interest in child psychology and particularly in psychoanalysis derived from a profound curiosity about human nature and two marked traits in her character: a strong practical tendency and a dislike of waste. In the wilderness of good intentions how much ill-directed and wasted effort would be avoided if we could start nearer the beginning, with tested knowledge and understanding of the drives and motivations behind the irrationalities of human behaviour. The value of Susan Isaacs' contribution to our knowledge in these fields is measurable by the patience and the insight with which she set about observing and recording the minute details of the activities of the group of twenty or so children who formed her experimental school at the Malting House, Cambridge.

'Out of that pioneering experiment grew her two classic works, *Intellectual Growth in Young Children* and *The Social Development of Young Children*, which, with her two smaller popular books, *The Children We Teach* and *The Nursery Years*, have been amongst the formative influences in the educational thought and practice of the last twenty years. Characteristically she turned aside in later years from what many regarded as her most valuable work in which she had achieved a unique authority, to deepen her own knowledge of psycho-analytic technique and theory which she believed indispensable to fruitful achievement in any study of human behaviour.

'To meet her in argument was to realize quickly her passion for fact and her disdain of improvization and loose thinking, a passion and a disdain comparable to that which inspired Beatrice Webb in her social investigations; and she could be pungently scornful of those who argued and behaved as though in any sphere of social or psychological research the last word had been spoken by a single great mind, whether it be Marx or her own revered leader, to whom she owed such profound allegiance, Freud.

'These were the known and public sides of her mind and character. Known only to her friends were her great sense of fun, her eager but generous competitiveness, her love and wide knowledge of birds and flowers, her love of music and poetry, and her devotion to the Scottish mountains. She undertook a great risk and endured considerable pain to travel north this summer that she might see her beloved Highlands again, knowing that she would be seeing them for the last time.

'It was in keeping with her outlook and her character that she should have asked that there should be no "speechmaking"

142

at her funeral, but only that some favourite pieces of music should be played and some poems read. Susan Isaacs had genius and greatness, but her epitaph might well be the last line of Francis Thompson's poem, "To My Godchild", the final stanza of which was read as she departed from us: "Look for me in the nurseries of heaven."'

7 · Her contribution to education

Above all else, Susan Isaacs has deepened immeasurably our understanding of children. In that respect, her contribution to psycho-analysis as well as to education is unquestioned. Dr Winnicott, with his genius for saying in the simplest of words things which convey profound meaning, says 'Psycho-analysis was strengthened by Susan and helped not to make too many silly mistakes about children.' The same might certainly be said about education and about child care and upbringing.

Though her work in psycho-analysis meant more to her than any other part of her professional life, Susan herself was convinced that she made no special contribution to it. She valued it partly just because she was so sure that there were others very far ahead of her in that field, from whom she could learn, and because the exploration of her patients' minds was always adding to her own knowledge and insight. It is probably true that her most significant contributions were to parents and teachers in educational practice and in bringing her clear and critical mind to bear on educational principles and psychology. Nevertheless, she was undoubtedly valued by psycho-analysts. Mrs Riviere, in a letter to Nathan Isaacs, said, 'We are missing her very sadly in our work as, indeed, I had long foreseen.' I have already mentioned the tributes of Dr Paula Heiman ('She had an enormous influence on the attitude to children') and of Dr Lois Munro: 'Colleagues who knew her in the field of psycho-analysis always hesitate and seem reluctant before they, on the whole, agree that perhaps she was right in saying that in their field she did not contribute anything actually original.'

Her main contribution to psycho-analytic theory was her ability to express and therefore clarify ideas rather than to initiate them. She gave great support to Melanie Klein and, through her constructive criticism, led her and others to clarify and establish their views on a more firm foundation. Her greatest contribution to psycho-analysis, however, was her interpretation of it in a way which made it intelligible and acceptable to a world outside. Where teachers and parents are concerned, it is probably true that she interpreted not only Dewey 'better than he inter-preted himself' but Melanie Klein also. Her contribution in that respect has meant that never again will teachers, parents, nurses, and all those who have to deal with children be cut off from the illumination of the child's emotional life which owes more to psycho-analysis than to any other field of inquiry. Through her own long and rigorous academic education she was also able to win the respect of other psychologists and to help very much in the cause about which she cared deeply, that of bringing together in the interests of children, what is revealed about them by different disciplines and methods of research. In a lecture given in 1938, she said: 'What I have been trying to do in this lecture is to indicate some of the trends in recent research into child psychology, and some of the extremely suggestive results of various studies affected by these influences, and to suggest in general that there is a growing convergence of method and of conclusions between all investigators who are honestly con-cerned with real and living human beings, whose approach is genuinely psychological. We are beginning to see an approxima-tion of clinical and of quantitative studies, which is bound to be immensely fruitful for the future.'

Sir Cyril Burt in reply to a letter in which I asked him for his views on Susan Isaacs' special contribution to psychology writes: 'I am sure she made a special contribution to Child Psychology. As so often happened, her books and articles were quickly read by her contemporaries and her ideas and influence have thus got incorporated in their writings and so passed on, and their origin forgotten. I think one of her chief contributions was an early and partial acceptance of the ideas about children *deduced* by Freud; a check on them by *first-hand* studies of young children, and a popularization of them in a modified and more acceptable form – so far as they applied to British children. I think her most important contributions were her studies of children at the Malting House School. I myself thought this a valuable investigation of gifted children at a very early age. . . . But both the methods and results were to a large extent applicable to the teaching of average children and were I think chiefly accepted from that point of view. Her work had started before Piaget's was known or published, and in my view was superior to, and much more exact than, his.

(*a*) It influenced methods of observing children and systematic- ally recording the results.
(*b*) It influenced the teaching of young children.
(*c*) The observations on the thinking and reasoning of young children showed that their potentialities were much greater than had previously been assumed.'

Sir Cyril Burt ascribes the rapid spread of her influence partly to the frequency with which her work was quoted both by Sir Percy Nunn and Professor Valentine, whose books were much read in training colleges for teachers, and also to her contributions to the Board of Education's Consultative Committee.

Susan Isaacs' great ability to reveal children to all kinds of people is written about so often and in so many ways that it is impossible to do more than quote a few examples.

Arnold Campbell, speaking for himself and also for the New Zealand teachers, said, 'She gave a revaluation, or rather an exposition, of the fascinating drama of the young child's emo- tional life and also showed us, on the intellectual side, that a child's mind would work very well in a child's world. She

showed teachers the whole rationale of the balance needed between freedom and control, healthy leaving alone and yet enough
support. No deeper child psychology was available before her
time to teachers, nor to parents, to help in bringing up their
children and she could speak to them because she recognized the
rights of parents and teachers too.'

Mary Maw, tutor to child-care courses for the Home Office,
writes: 'It has been said that Susan Isaacs, perhaps more than
anyone else in recent years, is responsible for ordinary people's
better understanding of young children. . . . She looked at children in the ordinary situations and relationships of daily life;
whole situations, not confined within artificial limits, not nar-
rowed by test requirements. The child's whole world was her
workshop, all he did and said – her raw materials. Nothing less
would suffice her for anything less would have fallen short of
truth. To a mind less competent, a vision less clear, the wealth
and variety of her material would have appeared overwhelming,
but her scientific approach was equal to her task and, as a result
of her systematic sorting of that material, reducing it to order
and using it to illustrate every aspect of children's development,
she produced, in two volumes [*Intellectual Growth in Young
Children* and *Social Development of Young Children*] an unrivalled
classic in the field of Child Psychology. . . .

'In her sensitive understanding of children's feelings, Dr Isaacs
is never unaware of the reality of the parents' problem. Implicit
in all her advice is recognition of the mutuality of the parent–
child relationship. It is a recognition rooted in her scientific
knowledge of the intricacies of the family pattern. It is, however,
far more than a reasoned intellectual appraisement, and herein
lies the genius of this part of her work: ordinary mothers' and
fathers' instant and confident acceptance of her teaching is due
even more to the genuine warmth of her wish to help them than
to her scientific accuracy. . . . It is natural to find Susan Isaacs
actively concerned for children whose satisfactory development
is handicapped in any way. Thus, when we turn our attention
from children brought up in the family setting to those less

fortunate ones who, for one reason or another, have never known, or have lost, their homes and parental care we find her giving evidence before the Curtis Committee. . . . Her evidence, set forth with typical logic and with deep concern, is unequalled in its clarity and human appeal. She felt that in order to make unmistakably clear just how much was involved in the loss of normal home life she must set forth in positive terms just what a good home embodies. Against this positive good she then set poignant examples of the evil that attends its disruption, and, finally, offered entirely practical suggestions for its mitigation. . . . It may be found in its entirety in *Childhood and After*. Many people feel that in this evidence Susan Isaacs epitomized her understanding of children and their needs, and that in the whole range of her writings it is unsurpassed. Implicit in it is recognition that in children's homes there must be staff fitted by temperament and adequately trained to understand the essential needs of children.'

Miss Maw was one of Susan's students in the Department of Child Development and can speak also of Susan's contribution to her students. She adds: 'Engaged as I am in training students for the care of children I am daily aware that all I teach rests upon what she taught me. I see now the purpose behind her planning of our course. Maybe, only a long time after, is it possible to appreciate fully the way in which her teaching equipped people for whatever work they subsequently took up.'

This reminds us that Susan's contribution is not contained only in her writings, valuable as they are, but in the lives and work of many people in many fields who, carrying with them what she contributed to their understanding, then go on to add their own contributions by observing the children and adapting to their needs and those of their own students. Her influence has spread far beyond those who were privileged to know her. Indeed, many of them are unaware of where the influences which had led them to look at children with new insight came from.

Miss Metcalfe Smith, another of Susan's past students, recalls a week-end meeting at Dartington Hall where in a large room with a very mixed audience of sixth form pupils, staff, students, and parents, including intellectuals and workers on the estate, Susan had kept them all spellbound with a talk on intellectual growth in young children, and she said that from the discussion which followed it was clear that everyone had enjoyed it enormously and learnt much.

The way in which Susan Isaacs' teaching has permeated into every sphere of those who work with children owes much to her ability to communicate on many different levels. To appreciate what she gave to our understanding of children, it is necessary to read her own writings. Selection is impossible because she saw the child whole in every aspect of his development and as fully human. She often said in her lectures that, by the end of the first year, the child showed that he could experience the whole range of human emotions in their simpler forms, even such complex ones as loss or grief; and she had a like respect for his powers of learning through his own experience, if he was in an environment which was physically and humanly suited to his stage of development.

Because of her awareness of the whole child, she could not be led astray by theories, however exciting, which left the real child out of account. She was perfectly balanced, as few people have been, between her awareness of the child's feelings and his thinking and learning, and always saw their relevance to and impact on each other. Neither did she ever forget the importance of his physical development and bodily needs. It was characteristic of her that once when someone expressed approval of sending evacuated children to a formal school, which they disliked, in order that they should like and appreciate their residential home, she said 'But how absurd! Children can't learn in those places.' No one who had studied with her would be tempted to forget that children cannot be really emotionally satisfied unless they can also learn, nor really learn unless their emotional needs are met.

Her great influence sprang from a combination of deep knowledge, sensitive observation and insight, robust common sense, and a sympathy which was extended not only to children but to those who care for and bring them up. She once said how pleasant it was to hear the friendly talk between children and their parents as they passed the window of her house on Primrose Hill and how seldom one heard the scolding and nagging which used to be so common. When I mentioned this to a friend I got an immediate response, 'I wish she could have known how much of that is due to her own work.' At the time of Susan's death, my sister (a mother and a children's nurse) wrote to me a sentence which delighted Nathan. 'To me she means lots and lots of unspanked babies and a lot more love in the world.' Susan's contribution above all else is that she brings the child to life so vividly in all aspects of his development that people understand and can sympathize with his point of view. What this has meant in the greater happiness of children can never be estimated but no account of Susan's contribution to us all must leave out her contribution to children themselves. Miss Dorothy May mentions that another of Susan's past students and friends, writing after Susan's death said: 'It is impossible to think of Susan Isaacs in the past tense. At her funeral we were bidden to look for her "in the nurseries of Heaven" . . . but it is no less sure that her spirit resides in many earthly nurseries and shines in happy freedom from the eyes of many children brought up not only with love, but with something of her own wise understanding.'

An obituary article published by the National Froebel Foundation Bulletin states: 'Only time will reveal how much we all owe to her teaching. The uniqueness of her contribution was due mainly to the fact that it was doubly-rooted, in a desire to help human beings, and a desire to find out what human beings were really like. She both loved and understood people. And the understanding also had two roots; she was an observer as well as a student. Her psychological learning was immense, and it was based not only on the laboratory and the library, but on field study of human beings. The Malting House School, an experiment in the education of young children to which she devoted four years, gave her the material for her most note-worthy educational writing. And her psycho-analytic practice gave her the insight into the social and emotional needs of children, which our earlier educational psychology had usually so pitifully neglected. She could show us the whole child, functioning as a whole, and she has stopped us from thinking of learning as the sole business of the school, while emotion is relegated to the home or the clinic.'

In the field of general psychology, Susan held an honoured place. At the time of her death Sir Cyril Burt wrote, 'Her loss to educational psychology will be quite irreparable.' In this field too she was very much at home and there was very little of the vast literature of general and educational psychology which she had not thoroughly assimilated. As Miss Clement Brown put it, she made a major contribution in being able to bring a combination of so many kinds of approach to the question of children. She described her, in debate and discussion, as making a penetrating analysis of logical conclusions and contributions to method as well as to content in discussions on research.

Susan would not have claimed to be the first or the only one to challenge some of the commonly held assumptions of her day, but she was very swift indeed to do so if they ran counter to what she knew to be true of children, and we owe it to her that some false assumptions and inadequate psychology disappeared from the teaching given in training colleges much earlier than they would have done without her.

She had a very strong influence in this country during the war when those in charge of young children were receiving advice arising from the theory of behaviourism in the narrower sense of that word. At a conference held for Ministry of Education inspectors who were being called to inspect the war-time nurseries, she was begged to attend, especially in order that her views should be heard by those who were likely to be advised to insist on rigid methods of 'habit training' which disregarded the child's feelings. Those who attended this conference told me how quietly and serenely she stood up to angry opposition from her opponents and relied solely on presenting evidence which was so unshakeable that no one present failed to be convinced by it. She could hold her own without producing unnecessary antagonism and, if it did arise, as on that occasion, was well in control of her temper. She undoubtedly emerged as the victor, though she felt she had lost some good opportunities of repartee. She made people think clearly about the whole nature and function of habit and dethroned it from its exalted position which had a profound effect on nursery school procedure.

Her attitude to 'behaviourism' is reflected in a letter which she wrote in 1934 to an American psychologist who sent her a friendly letter about her books and asked her to contribute an article to an American journal.

'Your plan of having each issue of the journal centred around a single topic seems to me an extremely good one, and I am very glad that you are dealing with this question of emotional development in childhood. I am also very delighted that you are able to deal with it from the point of view of the child's psychic experiences, and do not feel bound to deal only with his external behaviour. I know that it would be unjust to a great many workers in America to think of you all as concerning yourselves only with the description of external behaviour, but as that point of view looms so large in the American psychological literature which reaches us here, and makes such a song about itself, it is very easy for us in England to slip into thinking of American child psychologists as being adequately represented by the behaviourists, and those who feel happy only when they are measuring and drawing curves. I have, of course, the greatest respect for quantitative methods in their place, except when they attempt to make an exclusive claim to the title of being scientific, and refuse to recognize the absolute need to understand the inner psychic life of the child from his own point of view. It is, therefore, a great pleasure to see that you are prepared to deal with this problem of emotional development from this more significant point of view, and I shall be very delighted to contribute to your November issue.'

In 1935 an American psychologist wrote to her that he was proposing to plan a course of lectures and invited her comments upon what he thought should be said on the subject of personality. He said that 'personality, or the establishment of certain characteristic habits of feeling and acting, is the product of conditioning by environmental forces (chiefly the early family situation) acting upon original more or less undifferentiated drives which press for discharge, and which by becoming effectively discharged in specific types of situations erect these into "goals". This seems to me a general formula quite adequate (when developed) to encompass most of the very important psycho-analytic formulations on the topic; if you would care to venture a comment on it I should value the same very highly'.

Susan replied: 'I would agree in general with your statement about personality, save that I would emphasize rather more than you do in your phrasing the highly complex nature of the inner psychic life acting in response to environmental forces. I do not believe, that is to say, that the situation at any time after birth could be represented as simply as this: environmental forces, a to z, acting upon undifferentiated instinctual drives, l to n. At any time after the earliest few days the environmental forces do not act directly upon the primary drives but upon a series of highly complex psychic situations, a^1 to z^1, already built up in the mind of the child. This is a highly abstract statement, but I believe that the truths it represents are quite concrete and specific, and of the highest possible importance. To take a dramatic and rather extreme instance: a child of, say, seven or eight years, who has had a bad early environment of a kind that has given rise to a feeling of profound inner despair and guilt, will not necessarily be comforted and relieved and re-educated if at seven to eight years he now meets an environment that is entirely kind and tolerant. This may (I am of course speaking from instances) increase his inner sense of guilt and despair so greatly that he can only respond by being delinquent. This is where the work of actual analysis comes in, in getting behind the delinquent behaviour to the complex psychic structures which

153

lie behind it, and which give the environment at any later stage a special quality to the child himself which may be quite other from its objective characteristics.

'I can instance this endlessly, but perhaps it will suffice to show the direction in which I should want to add to your own admirable statement.'

It was characteristic of her that she did not overstate the position when she wished to challenge beliefs with which she did not agree, but began by looking at what was true and acceptable in the older theories.

In common of course with all the adherents of the newer schools of psychology, she was resistant to the ideas of totally separate faculties of the mind or separate instincts, but she helped those who were perplexed by the conflict between the idea of the 'libido' and the concept of instincts by the moderation and clarity with which she defined her position so that it was clear that she did not reject some of the earlier beliefs, but rather viewed them in a different way. Bewildered lecturers in training colleges were tremendously grateful for this clarity of exposition and realized that the new psychology did not mean that they needed to feel guilt for not immediately casting away what they had been trained to teach, but only to do some more flexible and realistic thinking. Her reference to instincts, written in 1934, illustrated her point of view very clearly.

'More complicated still are those inherited tendencies which may be broadly termed instincts – movements which are excited by outside stimuli and in which the whole body is concerned: each of them involves a tendency to recognize certain specific objects, and to make certain useful movements in regard to them. Although one or two of them may not be completely matured until much later, all the primitive instincts and emotions – weeping, smiling, laughing, fear, anger, disgust, sex, curiosity, self-assertion, self-submission, the protective instinct, the constructive instinct, and the like – emerge and manifest themselves during the first three or four years of life. In human beings the several instincts are not so sharply defined as they are in the lowlier animals: it is seldom easy to decide what is genuinely innate and instinctive, and what is due to early training or conditioning. As a result, psychologists differ considerably in the classification or human instincts which they have put forward. Perhaps it is wiser to regard the several instincts not as separate faculties or propensities, but rather as differentiated and related expressions of one single underlying vital impulse.'

Another challenge of Susan's to the orthodox psychology teaching of the time in teachers' training colleges is expressed by a comment of hers in her examiner's report on a candidate's work:

'I do wish we could give up teaching these dreary old theories of play. It seems to me pathetic that students spend so much time on discussing Schiller, Groos, etc., instead of (a) going direct to children at play and seeing for themselves what play does for children's development; and (b) making use of all the evidence available from child guidance clinics, etc., etc., as to the therapeutic value of play. There are so many positive facts that it is a waste of time to have recourse to theories that were put forward before adequate observations had been made.' Another 'orthodox' theory which Susan challenged was that of 'sense training'. In a letter to a would-be author, she writes:

'It is surely a great pity to perpetuate this old academic term, suggesting a narrow conception which you certainly do not hold. Wherever you use it you show that you are not thinking of "sense training" in the narrow Montessorian meaning, but are thinking of it as referring to the child's active interest in the world outside himself. But then why not say so? I don't believe that the child is ever interested in the development of his own senses. He is interested in things and the way they behave. He is interested in the colour of objects, the shape and sizes and mutual relations of objects, and what he can do with them. I think it is much better to say so, since your less well-informed readers may very well interpret you much more narrowly than you intend them to do.'

Another idea which she resisted, but which was held by many

people at that time, was that people could be classified into 'types'. In a review of Herbert Read's book *Education through Art*, which on the whole she greatly admired, she wrote:

'I do not feel the approach of the typologists to the problems of the human mind to be fruitful. I never have been able to sympathize with the attempt to pigeonhole human personalities into types. My own sense of underlying process in the human mind, my awareness of individuals, are both too strong. Moreover, my experience of the changes which character and personality may undergo in the work of psycho-analysis is too vivid. In analytic work one becomes so aware of the defensive function of the emphasis laid on particular aspects of personality: e.g. the extent to which the so-called "extravert" or "introvert" tendencies may be over-emphasized, the way in which sensation may be over-accentuated, or the value of "abstract" forms and qualities be underscored, all as defences against acute emotional conflicts. Once one has come to appreciate the dynamic interplay of these various functions, one cannot but find arid and profitless any pigeonholing of the living forces of the mind into fixed types.

'And in fact the typologists constantly warn us that their "types" are never found pure. Why not, then, express the facts in terms of process and tendency?

'To classify the products of the mind – such as the wonderful series of pictures with which this book is so generously illustrated – seems more legitimate, since here process and tendency have become crystallized into static form.'

Susan was also very much against the labelling of people as 'obsessional', 'paranoid', etc., and would warn her mental health students against picking up such terms which she felt prevented real thought about the people concerned and led to slick judgments. She was half amused and half indignant when a psychiatric social worker, old enough to have known better, referred to Winston Churchill, for whom Susan felt a deep admiration, as 'so adolescent'.

Susan's influence on the kind of psychology taught to students in training colleges was undoubtedly very great. Before her time very little was taught about children; the course consisted mainly of lectures on the nervous system, instincts, sentiments, and the learning process as such, but with little regard for children's actual learning. Animals were more frequently in the picture than people. Susan was concerned to make clear to her students not only in what ways human beings share the characteristics of animals, but also in what respects we differ from them, and she felt that young students of psychology could be misled rather than helped by too much emphasis either on animal psychology or the relation of psychology to the nervous system. She was very much in favour of beginning the teaching of child psychology by direct observation of the sayings and doings of children and by discussion of what children themselves revealed to the observers.

It is well known that she made certain criticisms of Piaget's early work, though she also respected it very much and agreed to some of his findings. Her main criticisms were centred in his method of taking evidence. She felt that when he put children into situations remote from their spontaneously discovered experiences and, moreover, often cross-questioned them, he puzzled them and prevented them from revealing their full capacity for thought. She felt that this led Piaget to conclusions that children were all at one level at one stage of their development, whereas in fact they might be at such a level in a test situation and at quite another when personally concerned and interested and when their experience was good enough to make a question comprehensible. Her criticism was not that there are no stages in development but rather of the rigidity of the idea that the child is at one stage all the time until he passes on completely to another, or that the adult never reverts to thinking in an infantile way!

She writes: 'There is, of course, some truth in the concept of stages of development brought about by a process of inner maturation. There are characteristic ways of mental response at different ages, and according to the growth of experience and knowledge. But to see these as a sort of metamorphosis at which definite changes occur in large part independently of experience, the previous stages being left behind, gives a distinctly false picture. We are all ego-centric, even in Piaget's technical sense; but here and there, experience has brought a little order into our thought, a little clear and certain knowledge into our equipment for handling the world.

'The interpretation of the child's beliefs, re the sun and moon, are a crucial illustration of this point. Children of a certain age think that the sun and moon follow them on their walks. One may call this "ego-centrism", etc., but before giving any mystic explanatory value to this term, one must remember that the sun *does* appear to do so. The illusion points not so much to mystic laws of mental development as to lack of actual experience and of organized knowledge. Given the condition of ignorance, ego-centrism will of course have sway; but the latter is not the *cause* of the former. And the later knowledge of the child is not only a function of his inner maturity, but at least equally, of his further experience. . . .

'In spite of all the precautions of the clinical method, we feel that forcing the child's thought out into the open in this way inevitably shows him at his lowest level. Allowing for the difference of information, which of us would not be thrown into confusion at having to make a shot at explaining "how the sun came" or "how the moon began"? If we think away our own organized knowledge and the methods of approach to similar problems which have been built out of that knowledge, can we imagine ourselves doing any better than the child? . . .

'To conclude, our reservations about the final value of Piaget's conclusions could be summed up thus: he tends to take the child on ground and by methods which put him at a disadvantage and give the adult a maximum advantage. He formalizes the differences thus revealed by calling them various "isms". By substantifying them and thus sharpening their contours, he dispenses himself from looking for likenesses and continuities. And, moreover, he idealizes the adult, taking him at his highest intellectual levels. These tendencies all converge to over emphasize and stereotype the contrast between the child and the adult, and to create far too sharp and even static a view of the various stages of development and the changes leading from one to another.'

Susan Isaacs did not, of course, live long enough to know all of Piaget's recent work which would have appealed to her much more strongly than his earlier experiments did. But she was by no means unappreciative of much of his early work and in sympathy with many of his findings to which she often paid tribute, as he, with like generosity, did to her work and to her criticisms.

Eileen Edwards, writing from Australia, says, 'Her own stress on the importance of the child's experience in determining how the child thinks is closer to the position which Piaget himself would now hold than was the case in 1930 when her book on intellectual development was published.'

However, as early as 1929, Susan had written: 'The importance and interest of these contributions of Piaget can hardly be over-estimated. He has not only added greatly to our store of facts about the child's belief and ways of thought; he has gone far to show how these hang together as a coherent psychological whole. No psychologist can afford to pass by either the great mass of data which Piaget offers, or his theoretical mode of marshalling the facts. And the philosopher will do well to look at the transformations through which his favourite themes pass in the process of development, and the curious analogies of these with the history of thought, which Piaget brings out.'

I have given only a few examples of how Susan Isaacs looked carefully and critically at some general psychological conceptions commonly held in her day and also at research methods, always from the point of view of how they did or did not fall in line with what has been learnt by careful observation of children in actual situations.

While she was fully aware of the importance of experimental studies with children, she insisted that these cannot lead to more than limited evidence and that the limitations must be defined. In a letter to a psychologist who asked her advice about an experimental research into the ability of children to accept criticism and make self-criticisms at certain ages, she writes: 'The only reserve I have about it is that the whole approach to the problem seems to imply that there is a development of self-criticism and power of receiving criticism of others, as such, which operates independently of *genuine* social situations. I don't say of course that there is not such development, but only emphasize that this is assumed by the method. These experimental situations are not real to the child, do you think? I feel that children could tolerate and make use of criticism in these situations, which are rather playfully removed from significant moments in ordinary life, who could not tolerate genuinely operating criticism, with all the underlying aggressive intention of criticism in real relations with their playmates or grown-ups. Of course I don't suggest that it is not worth while tracing the course of development under these conditions, and I am fully aware that you yourself would feel that these experimental conditions are not to be confused with the way in which criticism would operate in real life in their full setting of emotion and social relation. But it does seem to me that this needs to be brought out in the appraisement of the results, indeed I would like to see a study made of what relation, if any, could be discovered between the course of development in individual children or group of children as revealed by such an experiment as yours, on the one hand, and as shown by observational studies in real life – classroom, playground, home – on the other.'

In another letter to a teacher who had asked her advice about a proposed study of children's social behaviour, she wrote: 'One of the difficulties of a quantitative approach to social development in early life is the assumption that the mere number of itemized contacts is the important thing, as compared with general attitudes, which are not readily open to quantitative treatment. We know already that social life after five years is much more fully developed and stable than earlier. If it should turn out to be that the actual countable number of contacts is less, this could only be because social relationships are more sustained, not that the child is less sociable. After all, people can sustain real mutual awareness and contact sometimes without exchanging a word. This is one of the complexities of social development which makes it so difficult to express things in quantitative terms. In a fussy, anxious child, the number of separate contacts may be more just because he is insecure, whereas rather older and more socially developed children may work quietly side by side, or even with each other, with relatively few countable, but more sustained *items* of contact. Perhaps you will think about this difficulty? And the problem of finding a method to deal with it in the records.'

Again and again Susan Isaacs reminded us of how important it is in all studies to take account of how much more children can reveal to us in all aspects of their development if we observe them objectively in the situations of their everyday life. She would not have us rely for our knowledge of children entirely on tests and structured situations any more than she would advocate these as being the best situations to encourage young children to function at their highest level. She also had reservations about too much reliance on recording observations of children under particular selected headings, because of the close inter-relationship of their activities and the impact of the whole situation on anything which a young child may do or say. She had more sympathy with recording whole situations and analysing them afterwards, which she felt was much less likely to distort the evidence, though recording might have to be less detailed. However, while Susan's own preference was clearly for observational studies of young children in a natural setting, she was deeply interested also in sound experimental studies of such aspects of children's thinking, imagination, or performance as can be measured experimentally as, for example, Ruth Griffiths's *Study of Imagination in Early Childhood*, or Lois Murphy's *Study of Sympathy,* which employed a combination of observations in a natural setting with putting the children into single experimental situations too. She was fully sympathetic to my own researches, which were mainly of an experimental nature, and to those of many others, but she was very critical of claiming too much from any techniques which put children into artificial situations, particularly in work with children below an age when they could be expected to enjoy a test and therefore co-operate fully with the investigator.

Her seminars on methods of research with young children helped people to think realistically and set up investigations with care about the child's point of view and she taught people to be very critical of results claimed on so called 'research' when such precautions had not been taken. In this respect, she made a very real contribution to research methodology.

Second only to the understanding of children, and closely allied to it, was Susan Isaacs's contribution to education. In Chapter IV, on the Malting House School, I have emphasized that she installed play in the foremost position in the nursery and infant schools. Though she herself ascribed her educational principles to the influences of Froebel and Dewey, there is no doubt that she added fresh contributions to theirs. Froebel, though rightly described as 'the apostle of play', lacked the support of an organized body of psychological knowledge gained by research, and his observations of young children were coloured by his own philosophical and metaphysical ideas. Particularly in the later part of his life, he ascribed almost mystical values to the use of particular toys in particular ways, and sometimes failed to look at situations through the eyes of a child. For instance, he believed that a baby could attain to such an abstract idea as that of 'diversity in unity and unity in diversity' by playing with a ball because it was a single object with an infinite number of sides. Even Susan's respect for the powers of thought which are released in young children through the medium of play would not have credited them with so great an ability to come to such abstract conclusions. Moreover, though Froebel was far ahead of his time in the understanding of children, he tended, as Rousseau did, to idealize them. He was, therefore, unaware, as Susan so vividly *was* aware, of the need to permit and provide for sublimatory outlets for feelings of hate and aggression. Susan brought a much more objective and biological approach to her observations of children, and had respect for the real child's own wishes and feelings.

Dr Edna Oakshott wrote: 'Through the able exposition of her findings, the mystical approach to children, which had been for so long an obstacle to sound educational theory, was successfully challenged and the young child was brought into the perspective of human growth.'

Susan's criticisms of Montessori were largely based on the tendency of Dr Montessori to believe that if she gave 'freedom' to children they would respond in precisely the ways she expected, and indeed required. Dewey's principles and practice were nearer to Susan's own. She says in a letter to a writer from America: 'My own views have a much closer relation to the educational philosophy of Dewey than of Montessori. I don't quite understand why you think I am based on Montessori, since in my previous volume, *Intellectual Growth*, I made severe criticism of her views, and the whole of my *Social Development* runs counter to her views of the child's mind. Dewey, however, has always had a profound influence on my educational thought.'

She did more, however, for the education of the child under six, to whom Dewey had devoted less attention. Particularly, she explored much further the interests of quite young children in the world around them, and though she would have agreed that the source of many of the child's interests is in the home, she would not have expected that those of six-year-olds would be as narrowly confined to this as Dewey suggested – indeed, she found that well before the age of six, children's minds were reaching out to understand many other matters in a wider world. She went further than Dewey, in that in her own school, she did not so much 'plan projects' and thus present problems to children as investigate what their own individual purposes were and help them follow them up and solve their own problems. Nor did she assume that large groups of children would feel similar enthusiasm for one topic, and she was keenly aware of the need to provide for children whose intellectual interests might carry them much further than what would be reasonable to expect of more average or backward children.

I have already referred to the way in which she studied and made clear to others the true role of the teacher in supporting, while respecting, the child's discoveries, never cutting across his purposes by substituting her own, but ready to offer from her greater knowledge and experience whatever would help the child in his own quest for knowledge and bring him nearer to achieving his goals. I have also referred to her clarification of the balance needed by children between freedom to explore and express their feelings and the kind of supporting, firm, but not aggressive, control which they need to protect them, not only from physical dangers, but from the deep anxieties of being left without help in controlling their own aggressive impulses. In her pamphlet, *Psychological Aspects of Child Development*, Susan refers to 'the importance of a settled framework of control', in which she has clarified the minds of many progressive teachers who were in doubt about this question. She writes: 'If this real external control is mild and tempered, although firm and secure, it enables the child to master his aggressive impulses and learn to adapt his wishes to the real world. If he neither finds fulfilment of his phantastic dreads in the outer world (i.e. by severe discipline), nor is left at their mercy in his inner world by having no external support, but is slowly educated by a tempered, real control, mild and understanding and appropriate to each situation as it arises, he is led forward on the path of real achievement.'

Susan Isaacs' deep comprehension of the principles of progressive education, in its best sense of the word, has implications far beyond the nursery and infant school. Though the word 'play' ceases to be appropriate as children grow older and begin to make a distinction in their own minds between work and play, the principle of basing the education we offer upon the purposes and discoveries of the learner would, if accepted, lead to genuine learning and understanding at all stages of education. Indeed, these are precisely the principles followed by Susan in her own education of her students: as Dr Lois Munro put it, 'supporting their discoveries and being a "container of their questing"', and she imparted these same ideas to those of her students who were to train others. Her influence is reaching many junior schools and even some secondary schools today; she lived to see its effect on nursery and infant schools. The Froebel Bulletin (1948) from which I have already quoted ends with the words:

'Changes in our schools come very slowly. Old ways of thinking have become set not only in ourselves, but crystallized in our buildings, our apparatus, our school books, our methods. But at any rate desire for change is growing, and more and more teachers are being trained in the newer, freer ways. In these new ways with young children, Susan Isaacs had more part than any person of our generation in this country.'

As was to be expected, Susan lent the weight of her influence against anything which might stand between children and what she was convinced was real education. The following letter illustrates her forthright criticisms of education as she saw it in 1936. It would be well to consider how far some of her criticisms are still justified and whether, when they are not, we owe something to her that improvements have taken place. The letter is written to Max Nicholson (Political and Economic Planning) who, at the suggestion of Mr. Leonard Elmhirst of Dartington Hall, had written to ask for her comments on a proposed memorandum.

'I was extremely interested in the analysis of the problem of government in modern social life and the necessary adjustment to scientific conditions. I am entirely in agreement with the suggestion that one of the focal points of the problem is education; and the training of teachers is an essential key. I would emphasize further the following points: (a) the imperative need to lessen the stranglehold of the universities through the mechanism of the school certificate, and hence the scholarship exam at eleven plus, on the education of young children. My own experience in recent years in contact with infant and junior schools suggests that all educational values are distorted through the need to prepare children for these exams. Even with children at four and five years of age, people are already beginning to think about the scholarship exam, and it is extremely hard to humanize the education of even the very young because of this. (b) Specifically, we teach reading and writing and the formal arts far too early, substituting sterile attempts to compose with the pen for living communication by word of mouth. The time that is spent in formal work on the three R's would be far better employed in allowing the children to pursue the activities they so much seek connected with the business of living – washing, cooking, cleaning, searching out facts about the way the home is kept going and the life of the town maintained. The ordinary child of five to nine years of age is civically minded in the sense that he is interested in all those activities of the home and the town (or the country), the subject-matter of the social and physical sciences: physics, chemistry, geography, economics, etc. These activities are the natural starting point for his education, and today the school deliberately deadens his interest in these things and idolatrizes the formal tools of learning. It is little wonder that children of the school leaving age cease to take any interest in geography, economics, literature, social administration, etc. There is an extraordinary disproportion between the time and trouble put into teaching children to read and write at far too early an age and our concern with the real use of these things to serve personal and social life.

'My special point here, therefore, is that we have not only to consider the teaching of children in the senior and secondary schools, but also in the infant and junior periods. It is in the infant and junior school that we begin to go wrong so disastrously, and we can never retrieve the mistakes we make at that critical period by even the most skilful teaching in the adolescent years.

'I agree that teachers should be trained so as to give them knowledge and insight into public affairs, with more attention to the social sciences throughout the curriculum. But (a) a very important lever in these studies is the study of the child himself. The time available for direct attention to child psychology and

166

child welfare in all its aspects is far too small in the curriculum of the training college student at present; and (b) this is so partly because students are only half educated when they enter upon their professional courses. A large part of their time in the training colleges has to be given to completing their ordinary academic qualifications. The suggestion that they should have a period of time away from the schools altogether, in some form of travel or practical life, is an excellent one. But I would also urge that the study of academic subjects – history, literature, etc., should be subordinated to the broad study of the needs of children and of the social functions which serve those needs.'

Susan Isaacs was always a firm supporter of nursery school education, the most neglected part of our education system. She did much to convince people that not only were nursery schools essential if we are to promote full growth and development for children living under conditions of poverty, overcrowding, or other forms of stress, but also that they offered further opportunities for learning and developing rich social relationships than even the best of homes can normally offer without their help. She valued nursery schools as much for their service to children of very high intelligence as for what they could give to those who were backward and inarticulate. Though she convinced many people, we cannot claim that as yet all her work and effort has resulted in a generous provision of these schools. Susan Isaacs was interested in all children, but her deepest concern of all was for the very young child. This country continues to feel more concern about raising the school leaving age than for providing nursery schools, and it seems it is only in war time that our consciences are really stirred about making provision for young children. Susan Isaacs' enthusiasm for nursery school education was so great that people tended to identify her and her department at the university entirely with the education of children under five and, as her successor, it took me nearly twenty years before I could really convince people that the Department of Child Development had never actually thus limited its functions.

I was told again and again that Susan Isaacs had trained *only* nursery school teachers, whereas in fact there was not even one in her first group of students, and there never was a time when she did not have a majority of people who taught children up to the ages of seven or eleven years, and sometimes older than that. She did, however, believe very strongly that good nursery school education was the right foundation both for national education and for the studies of her students, whatever age they were teaching or going to teach, and she rejoiced in the appointment of one of her most able first students, Miss Dorothy May, to a nursery school superintendent's post in London when she completed her course in the department. If Susan Isaacs failed to get nursery schools provided on the scale she would have wished, at least she got them respected. Miss Margaret Metcalfe Smith from the University of Leeds (also one of Susan's much valued first students), writes, 'She helped to put good education of young children "on the map", as something very significant and worthy of intellectual effort of the highest kind – research, university teaching, and a university department.'

Susan will be remembered as a teacher and supporter of the 'progressive' or 'liberal' type of education, for which it is so difficult to find an adequate name, unless we describe it rather laboriously as the kind of education which is based on following up and providing for the satisfaction of children's interests, aiding their discoveries, and helping them to achieve their own purposes, while also providing an environment which will afford rich and valuable opportunities for their growth and development! As Arnold Campbell puts it: 'She was basically a liberal educationalist, but she did not antagonize the formalists.' Hannah Steinberg, another admirer of her work, both expands and explains the reason for his statement: 'She was, above all, a pioneer and as such always a little ahead of her time; but in her the enthusiasm of inquiry and adventure was wisely tempered with the caution of a background of sound practice and knowledge of theory – an unusual combination which enabled her both to take account of what was best in the existing ways, and from there to advance further and make her own original contribution.'

She had a very deep respect and sympathy for the work of teachers and made it clear that their own contribution to children was so vital that they must not spoil it by confusing their role with that of the psycho-therapist, as at one stage some of them were tempted to try to do. She explained to teachers very clearly in what respects the two roles are different and how important it is to children to enjoy the therapeutic relationship in the real world with a wise and sympathetic teacher. She often referred to the pleasure of being taught by a good teacher and she spoke to them as one who had been herself a teacher, and indeed who continued to be one throughout her life. They were quick to appreciate her realistic understanding of their function and their needs for help in their exacting profession. Miss E. M. Ingram, who devoted her whole professional life to the teaching of children throughout the full range of the primary school, expresses the viewpoint of the teacher:

'She made a "bridge" for teachers between the work of educational theorists and classroom principles and practice today. She understood and conveyed the relevance to us of the contributions of Froebel, Dewey, Piaget, Montessori, and above all Freud. The effect of their work was integrated by her own thought so that she could really use it all to increase people's understanding of children.

'She respected teachers but did not feel it was necessary to make them all study the complete theoretical writings of all these people. She wanted to give them the fruits of her own study of them.

'She saw the need to go further even than Dewey saw it, for example, to go deeper into many aspects of the environment, such as physiology.

'She *released* teachers and set them free to watch how children unfolded and really convinced them of what Froebel said – that the child was not a bad person who needed to be changed but a good one who needed to unfold. She had so assimilated this point of view and the other fruits of her studies that teachers often ascribed the whole of the ideas to her. She never took an idea without something happening inside her, and this caused other teachers to do likewise. Her terrific vibrance to people and experience made her a tremendous source of *ideas*. Her influence was like a stone dropped into a pool. She stirred the waters and others could bathe in them. Her work appeals not only to the very intellectual reader, as Dewey on the whole does. Susan's writing is so tremendously alive that it carries the reader along with her. She was truly scientific. Her work is based on observation not "ologys". She was looking at children, working with them, and writes straight from that experience. She shows every detail to be of importance and that means more than a general idea. She showed teachers how to distil the relevance of details, however small, and interpreted these so that they could see their relevance. This showed headteachers how to help their staffs.'

It might be said, and Susan would have agreed, that she did not originate any very new educational method. Indeed, it is probable that those who have helped us most in education have not done this by originating methods, but by contributing to our thought. Dewey was very anxious that there should never be 'a Dewey method', and in that he showed his wisdom. Susan undoubtedly made an original contribution to our thoughts about education because of the inspired way in which she assimilated and related so much knowledge from very varied fields of deep and intensive study and from her perceptive observation and practical experience. Where she was undoubtedly unique was in her ability to bring all that was relevant from all she knew and understood so well to bear upon any specific practical situation, as can be clearly seen in such contributions as her paper on 'Child Psychology and the Accident Problem' and in countless other of her published and unpublished lectures and letters.

She has transformed the lives of many children in school and the whole concept of education for many teachers. Whether her name will appear in future textbooks on the history of 'Education' I do not know, but it deserves to be there. It is not necessary for an architect to make the bricks before we ascribe the credit of a building to him; and Susan has assembled her knowledge and wisdom in ways which have already had a very great impact upon the education of young children.

On this last page of my manuscript (appendices don't count) I want to give two quotations, the first from an article in the *Times*:

'Susan Isaacs had a unique combination of gifts. Her high intelligence and eager scientific interests were united with deep humanity and natural insight. This last was greatly enhanced by her command of both analytical and general psychology. She could throw new light on the true needs and interests of children, which must underlie all real education, and she could expound her theories persuasively at all levels, from that of the parent or teacher with little technical psychology to that of the trained expert. The result has been that her teaching has probably influenced educational theory and practice in this country more than that of any living person.'

In the report on the *Post-primary School Curriculum* (published by the New Zealand Department of Education in 1944), there is a passage from Susan Isaacs' book, *The Children We Teach*, which not only expresses what she held to be the aim of education, but is also a fitting description of her own personality.

'In the words of one writer, "The aim of modern education is to create people who are not only self-disciplined and free in spirit, gifted in work and in enjoyment, worthy and desirable as persons, but also responsible and generous in social life, able to give and take freely from others, willing to serve social ends and to lose themselves in social purposes greater than themselves."'

Appendices and Bibliography

APPENDIX I

I took the following notes at a lecture given by Susan Isaacs at the special request of the students taking the course in mental health at the London School of Economics. They asked her to tell them what she thought normal child development would lead to in the characteristics of a 'normal adult'. Since this (unpublished) lecture aroused much interest, and also illustrates Susan's views, which are better known in relation to children than to adults, it seemed perhaps of interest to include it here.

In this lecture I shall consider both the question of norms of development in the adult and the question of what has life to do for us as individuals.

To begin with this second question: first, life must provide us with instinctual satisfactions. These need not all be directly expressed. A vast amount of instinctual life can be satisfied indirectly in work, art and pleasure.

Satisfactions are not all sexual. Hate and aggressiveness need satisfaction too. These are demanded in war but also in normal life. Some professions contain sublimated aggression – surgery, demolition, sawing, blasting. Criticism is an expression of aggressiveness. Our pleasure in the mastery of objects arises primarily from the hate impulses: seafaring, architecture, etc., involve mastery. So does all tackling of difficulties.

Secondly, we need to find ways in which conflict about primitive drives can be dealt with and to find reassurances about anxieties, conflict, and guilt.

Thirdly, life has to help us to adjust to the reality of nature and of society.

Norms. We use the term 'normal' in two senses. In one sense we mean that 'normal' stands for the majority of men and women. In another sense we use it as if it were an absolute ideal of perfect development. In this lecture the term will be used in the first sense. It is better for us not to have too ideal a notion of what is normal. The great majority of people are full of imperfections. Life only provides for our needs to a certain extent. It never gives us 100 per cent satisfaction. Therefore adaptation to reality comes in. Normality means adaptation to psychical reality. We must learn: first, tolerance of our own guilt and anxiety, and second, tolerance of people as they are. Parents need to put up with children as they are, not as they wish them to be.

Efficiency. If too much energy is used on conflict it is not free for work and social contacts.

Happiness. For real happiness we must be able to admit sorrow, guilt, etc. We must swing between these states when there is real cause for it, but not exaggeratedly.

Balance consists of an equilibrium of many moving forces. Balance is maintained with greater and lesser ease. There is a limit to most people's balance. Change of mood is normal with real cause. If exaggerated it is abnormal. Changes in adult life demand flexibility. We should be able to accept changes and distribute our satisfaction. For example, we can, if normal, be both sociable and in love, except at special times (for example, the honeymoon). We should be able to love friends of the same sex. The purely heterosexual is very insecure. We should be able to work happily with both sexes. Balance should also be maintained between work and leisure (except at special times). People who can *only* work are not normal nor are those who can get no pleasure from work. We should be willing to accept the limitations imposed by life, to select and to abide by our choice. Neurosis expresses inner conflicts. A certain amount of neurotic symptom is normal. It is a matter of degree. Most people have some neurotic habits, nail biting, chewing gum, smoking. We all do something which shows inner conflict. Avoidance of certain objects – dislikes of certain food. Ways of travel – tube versus bus, etc. Dress is bound to express us. Eating habits, sleeping habits. Hours and methods of work – night and morning. We must be able to express our neurosis. (Daisy Bates, who worked in Australia in the early part of this century lived with the aborigines but never changed her Victorian dress, that was how she kept herself English.)

Avoid labelling people: 'Obsessional', etc. No one is purely normal and few are purely abnormal. A degree of repression is normal and gives a sense of 'being on top of the world' and able to cope with things.

Denial of our own feelings *can* be normal, e.g. in air raids.

Orderliness (within limits) is normal.

Giving, self-sacrifice in a worthy cause.

Marriage. If married we should be able to experience both bodily pleasure and psychic union with the loved person. Whether married or not we should be able to give love and win love. This is a very deep need. Some reassurance about this is needed but we should not need *constant* reassurance (see *Love, Hate and Reparation* – Riviere and Klein).

Parenthood. If we are parents we should experience pleasure both in our own satisfaction and in the development of the child. On the deeper levels, pleasure of mother in son may be that it makes up for not being a boy – in a daughter that she brings reassurances about her feelings towards her mother. It is normal to feel some triumph about marriage and parenthood and some anxiety too. The man is reassured about his potency and the woman about her capacity for having children. Sources of adult conflicts are in infancy. There is interplay between emotional and intellectual and psychic life and the environment. Creative impulses are as real as the destructive. As in early life there is complex interplay between them.

Summary

Maturity is a moving and changing thing. It consists of maintaining an intricate balance. It is achieved during the stormy periods of infancy and early childhood, the more peaceful outward gazing middle years, and the re-orientation of adolescence.

No one is purely normal and few are purely abnormal. Army psychiatrists found in every case some degree of neurosis. It has been said that a normal person is one who can admit and put up with his neuroses. (This is not quite the right balance but pretty true on the whole.)

APPENDIX II

Report made by Susan Isaacs to Sir Fred Clarke on the Department of Child Development (February 1939)

Observations on the work and organization of the department

(1) The headship of the department is a half-time appointment; but the actual work of the department is full-time, the students attending lectures and seminars at the Institute, schools, and clinics on five full days per week.

(2) I myself give one lecture and take three seminars per week throughout the academic year.

(3) In teaching the students, I also enjoy the assistance of Professor Hamley (one seminar for two terms); Professor Samson Wright (six lectures); Dr Shepherd (six lectures); and Dr Winnicott (four lectures), together with the staff of the North Western Child Guidance Clinic, where each student attends for eighty hours during the session. In addition, students attend the two main lecture courses for Diploma Students, Principles of Teaching and Educational Psychology; and a certain number attend the laboratory discussion (Professor Hamley, Dr Smith, and Dr Fleming).

(4) The organization of the work of the students as a whole (discussions, observations in schools, and play-centres, visits to various institutions for infant welfare, etc.) is in my hands. I attend to all the visits to nursery schools and many institutions, but as regards visits to infant, junior, and senior schools, I have the kind assistance of Mr Harrison and Miss Usher Smith.

(5) The tutorial work with the students is entirely in my hands. This year there are twenty full-time students, as well as eight to ten part-time, all of whom have access to me when they wish, for discussing personal or professional problems, papers written for seminars, the preparation of theses, etc. (Several students undertake serious theses during the year, although this is voluntary.)

The part-time students often involve a good deal of responsibility, often coming to England from abroad for a special purpose, with special things they wish to learn and to discuss, e.g. I have this year received a student from Holland for two terms, who is writing a thesis for a special purpose in her own country and has asked for constant help.

As all my students are mature and experienced people not working for an examination, they do not require such constant nursing as diploma students need. On the other hand, they are so actively interested in their work and so much aware of the technical and human problems arising that they actually seek and enjoy a large amount of time in personal discussion.

(6) Moreover, since a large proportion of them each year come from abroad (America, Canada, New Zealand, Australia, Holland, Austria, Palestine, etc.), and have few if any friends in this country, I feel no little social responsibility for them. I am accustomed to receive the group as a whole socially once a week for 1–2 hours; formerly in my own home, now in my own room in the new building. This is in addition to other evening occasions for individual students or the whole group.

(7) In addition to students taking the ordinary courses for the department there is always a small number (two to four) of *research* students working for higher degrees in psychology; for these I have sole responsibility. Both Professor Hamley and Dr Smith have, however, been extremely generous in giving help to my research students.

I find myself able to see research students only in the evenings at home, as the pressure of appointments in the afternoons is too great.

(8) Beginning this session there is now another special group of students who are working for the Trainer's Diploma of the National Froebel Union. These students, three in number this year, take the whole of the ordinary course of the department, together with one or two of the special methods seminars of the diploma students, by the kind co-operation of other tutors (this year, Mr Jefferies and Dr Gurrey). Each of these students has a thesis to prepare for examination, involving much time for discussion and criticism.

This tutorial work, too, falls to me and has to be carried on at my home in the evenings.

These N.F.U. students also require special arrangements for practical work – in supervising the school practice of students in training, in conducting seminars and giving lectures to students.

I have also agreed to conduct their examination in psychology and principles of education – as part of my ordinary work, not at a special examiner's fee.

(9) A new development in the work of the department, the play room for children between 2 and 4 years, involves a good deal of organization and supervision. A small group of children now attends each morning during the university terms, in charge of a trained nursery school teacher who is also a student in the department. As far as my work is concerned, parents have to be interviewed, the group at play visited, equipment ordered, the progress of children discussed with the play room teacher, and reports made to parents. Students' observations and records are also considered and discussed.

As another example of the normal organizing work we are planning an arrangement with a senior girls' school, by which chosen girls will attend for a given period in the play room, helping with the routine care and receiving guidance and teaching in the handling of the children. This plan has involved, or will involve, correspondence and interviews with the Board's inspectors, the headmistress, and the girls.

(10) I interview all prospective students for the department and deal with all correspondence, other than the simple distribution of the descriptive leaflet. In addition to the formal statement given to each student at the end of her year as to satisfactory attendance and work, many students need testimonials and supporting references when applying for new appointments.

(11) The bulk of the correspondence of the department, however, has to do with the great volume of advisory work of one sort and another which is constantly carried on. The width and geographical distribution of this work makes it impossible to illustrate; but it could be said that in one capacity or another, the department is constantly functioning as an adviser in technical problems of child psychology or nursery education, and the training or appointment of teachers, in many parts of the world.

(12) In the same way, a large amount of time is spent in interviewing distinguished psychologists or responsible educators and child guidance workers from overseas, who wish to discuss specific problems with me. Sometimes these are people passing through London who take up an afternoon for discussion. Sometimes, such people come to London specially for this purpose, and spend anything from a week to a month or a term in the department with many separate occasions for talk. I look upon this as one of the most valuable spheres of influence for the department; but it consumes a great deal of time. (In particular, there is an increasing tendency for child psychologists and educationists from America to come to the department in this way.)

But many people from this country also come to discuss specific problems (Safety First Association, Film Institute, Speech Institute, Nursery School Association, National Froebel Union, and organizations dealing with refugee children, are recent instances.)

(13) The prestige of the department leads to my being asked to serve on a great many committees. Many of these I am obliged to refuse. But those I do accept take a heavy toll of time.

Committees

Member of Editorial Board (Home and School Council).
Member of Executive Committee (Home and School Council).
Member of Editorial Board (Association of Maternity and Infant Welfare Centres).
Member of General Committee (Nursery School Association).
Examiner in Educational Psychology (Diploma of Nursing).
Examiner for Central Examination (Association of Nursery Training Colleges).

(14) *Editing*

(1) I am on the Editorial Boards of :
British Journal of Psychology
British Journal of Medical Psychology
British Journal of Educational Psychology

(2) I am editing a series of pamphlets, 'Concerning Children', published by The Home and School Council, (ten pamphlets now published).

(3) I am editing a series of handbooks, 'Contributions to Modern Education', published by Methuen.
Now published:
The New Era in the Junior School, by E. B. Warr
The Children's Play Centre, by D. E. M. Gardner
Play in the Infants' School, by E. R. Boyce
The Human Problem in Schools, by M. Milner.

(4) Each month I reply to letters from parents and teachers, dealing with specific problems, in the monthly journal *Home and School* – I am also a member of the Magazine Committee.

N.B. All the above activities arise from my work and position as Head of the Department of Child Development – even my membership of the Committee of the Medical Section of the British Psychological Society. I was specifically invited as representing child psychology. I have not included paid examinerships for London and other universities, nor any of the work I do in connection with the London Clinic of Psycho-Analysis.

APPENDIX III

Summary of Susan Isaacs' Career

Graduate Scholar, University of Manchester, 1912.

Lecturer in Psychology, Darlington Training College, 1913–14.

Lecturer in Logic, University of Manchester, 1914–15.

Tutor for tutorial classes in Psychology, University of London, 1916–33.

Principal, Malting House School, Cambridge, 1924–27.

Research Assistant, Department of Psychology, University College, from 1932.

Various courses in Psychology for London County Council, Kent Education Committee, Morley College, etc.

Honorary Joint Secretary, Education Section, British Psychological Society, 1919–21.

Honorary Secretary, Committee for Research in Education, British Psychological Society, 1921–27.

Chairman, Education Section, British Psychological Society, 1928–31.

Fellow of Royal Anthropological Institute from 1923.

Member of British Psycho-Analytical Society from 1923.

Member of Council, National Institute of Industrial Psychology, 1921–29.

Member of Advisory Committee for Carnegie experiment in Vocational Guidance, National Institute of Industrial Psychology, 1923–31.

Assistant Editor, *British Journal of Psychology* from 1921.

Editorial Board, *British Journal of Educational Psychology* from 1931.

Member of staff of the London Clinic of Psycho-analysis, 1931.

Head of the Department of Child Development, University of
London Institute of Education, 1933–43.

Member of Training Committee of the London Clinic of Psycho-
analysis, 1944.

Member of Council of the London Clinic of Psycho-analysis,
1946.

1916 'Authority and Freedom', *Parents' Review*, 17.
1918 'Analysis of the Spelling Process', *Journal of Experimental Pedagogy*, 4.
1920 'The Present Attitude of Employees to Industrial Psychology', *British Journal of Psychology*, 10.
1921 'Science and Human Values in Industry', *The Co-operative Educator*, January 1921.
An Introduction to Psychology, London: Methuen. New York: Dodd, Mead & Co.
1923 'A Note on Sex Differences from the Psycho-Analytical Point of View', *British Journal of Medical Psychology*, 3, 288–308.
'Conflict and Dream', *The Highway*, May, 1923.
1927 'Penis-Faeces-Child', *International Journal of Psycho-Analysis*, 8, i, 74–76.
'The Function of the School for the Young Child', *Forum of Education*, 5.
1928 'The Mental Hygiene of the Pre-school Child', *British Journal of Medical Psychology*, 8, iii (re-printed in *Childhood and After*).
1929– Under pseudonym 'Ursula Wise' replied to correspond-
1936 ence in *The Nursery World*.
1929 'Some Reflections on Corporal Punishment', *The New Era*, July, 1929.
'Privation and Guilt', *International Journal of Psycho-Analysis*, 10, ii and iii, 335–47 (reprinted in *Childhood and After*).
'The Infant's Mind in the First Year of Life', five articles, *The Nursery World*, 8.
'The Child's Conception of the World', *Mind*, 38.

'Critical Review of Piaget', *Journal of Genetic Psychology*, 36.
'The Biological Interests of Young Children', *Forum of Education*, 1929, 7, and 1930, 8.
The Nursery Years, London: Routledge.
1930 *Intellectual Growth in Young Children*, London: Routledge.
'What the Nursery School can do for Young Children', *The Highway*, February, 1930.
'The Psychologist in Child Welfare', *Mother and Child*, I.
'The Experimental Construction of an Environment Optimal for Mental Growth', *A Handbook of Child Psychology*, edited by Carl Murchison, Clark University Press.
1930 *Health and Education in the Nursery* (with Dr Victoria M. Bennett), London: Routledge.
'The Humane Education of Young Children', *Report of the XIXth Annual Conference of Educational Associations*, 1931.
'A Brief Contribution to the Social Psychology of Young Children', *Journal de Psychologie*.
1931 'The Education of Children Under Seven Years', *British Journal of Educational Psychology*, Volume I, Part III, 1931.
1932 'Some Notes on the Incidence of Neurotic Difficulties in Young Children', *British Journal of Educational Psychology*, 2.
The Children We Teach, London: University of London Press.
1933 *Social Development of Young Children*, London: Routledge.
'The Psychology of the Two-Year-Old', *Mother and Child*, October, 1933.
'Original Sin', *Twentieth Century*, 1933.
Article entitled 'Intellectual Growth in Young Children', *Report of the Summer Short Course for Teachers of Physical Teaching of the Blind*, July, 1933.
1934 (Jointly with Professor Burt): 'Emotional Development up to the Age of Seven Plus', Appendix III, *Report on Infant and Nursery Schools*, pp. 244–51.

1934   'Rebellious Children', *Mother and Child*, 3, 1934.

'Critical Notice of J. Piaget', *The Moral Judgement of the Child*, January, 1934.

Mental Hygiene, 'Preventive Measures in Childhood', *Proceedings of the Royal Society of Medicine*, 1934.

'Rebellious and Defiant Children' (a public lecture delivered under the auspices of the Institute of Psycho-Analysis, first published in 1948 in *Childhood and After*, pp. 23–25).

'Property and Possessiveness' (a symposium 12 xii 34, with Ian D. Suttie, Morris Ginsberg, and T. H. Marshall), *British Journal of Medical Psychology*, 1936, 15, i, 64–78 (reprinted in *Childhood and After*, pp. 36–46).

1935   'Bad Habits', *International Journal of Psycho-Analysis*, 16, iv, 446–54.

The Psychological Aspects of Child Development, 1936, London: Evans Bros., and in *Yearbook of Education*, 1935.

1936   'Habit', Chapter in *On the Bringing Up of Children*, edited by John Rickman, London: Kegan Paul.

The Educational Guidance of the School Child, Evans Bros.

Testing Development, 'Personal Freedom and Family Life', *The New Era*, September, 1936.

1937   'Security for Young Children', *Child Study*, U.S.A., November, 1937.

'The Educational Value of the Nursery School', London: The Nursery School Association of Great Britain, first edition 1937, second 1938 (reprinted in *Childhood and After*, pp. 47–73).

1938   'Child Psychology and the Accident Problem' (reprinted in *Childhood and Youth*, 1950).

'Recent Advances in the Psychology of Young Children' (an address to the Education Section of the British Psychological Society at the XXVI Annual Conference of Educational Associations, 1938. Reprinted from the report of the Conference in *Childhood and After*, pp. 74–88).

'"Safety First" Examined', *Home and School*, October, 1938.

1939   'Modifications of the Ego through the work of Analysis' (a revised version of a paper read at a Symposium at the Joint Meeting of the British and French Psycho-Analytical Societies, Paris, 30th April, 1939, appearing in *Childhood and After*, pp. 89–108).

'A Special Mechanism in a Schizoid Boy', *International Journal of Psycho-analysis*, 20, iii and iv, 333–9 (reprinted in *Childhood and After*, pp. 122–8).

'Criteria for Interpretation' (Paris Psycho-Analytical Congress, 1938), *International Journal of Psycho-Analysis*, 20, ii, 148–60 (reprinted in *Childhood and After*, pp. 109–21).

1940   'The Uprooted Child', *The New Era*, March, 1940.

'Temper Tantrums in Early Childhood in their Relation to Internal Objects' (Paris Psycho-Analytical Congress, 1938), *International Journal of Psycho-Analysis*, 21, iii, 280–93 (reprinted in *Childhood and After*, pp. 129–42).

1941   *The Cambridge Evacuation Survey*, London: Methuen, edited by Susan Isaacs, S. Clement Brown, and R. H. Thouless.

1942   *The Family in a World at War*.

1943   'An Acute Psychotic Anxiety Occurring in a Boy of Four Years', *International Journal of Psycho-Analysis*, 24, i, 13–32 (expanded version of paper read to British Psycho-Analytical Society, 1938, reprinted in *Childhood and After*, pp. 143–85).

1945   '"Notes on Metapsychology as Process Theory": Some Comments', *International Journal of Psycho-Analysis*, 26, i, 58–62.

'Fatherless Children', in *New Education Fellowship Monograph No. 8*, edited by Peggy Volkov, reprinted in *Childhood and After*, pp. 186–207.

'Children in Institutions' (a Memorandum presented to the Home Office Care of Children Committee, 1945, first published as a whole in *Childhood and After*, pp. 208–38).

1947   Part of the above under the title 'The Essential Needs of Children' was published both in the *New Era* and *Childhood and Youth*.

1948   *Childhood and After*, Routledge and Kegan Paul.

'The Nature and Function of Phantasy', *International Journal of Psycho-Analysis*, 29, ii, 73–97 (contained also in the book *Developments in Psycho-Analysis* by Klein *et al.*, The Hogarth Press, 1952).

Troubles of Children and Parents, London: Methuen.